JOSEPH NYOMARKAY

CHARISMA AND FACTIONALISM
in the NAZI PARTY

Minneapolis
UNIVERSITY OF MINNESOTA PRESS

Library of Congress Catalog Card Number: 67-21015

PUBLISHED IN GREAT BRITAIN, INDIA, AND PAKISTAN BY THE OXFORD
UNIVERSITY PRESS, LONDON, BOMBAY, AND KARACHI, AND IN CANADA
BY THE COPP CLARK PUBLISHING CO. LIMITED, TORONTO

Part of Chapter V, "The Working Association of the North and West,"
pp. 71–89, has been published as "Factionalism in the National Socialist German Worker's Party, 1925–1926: The Myth and Reality of the
'Northern Faction,'" and is reprinted with permission from the *Political Science Quarterly*, Vol. LXX, No. 1 (March, 1965), pp. 22–47.

Table of Contents

Charisma and Factionalism
in the Nazi Party

WE LIVE in an age of the masses. But the future does not belong to the masses, but to him who fills them with an organic life. The new century belongs to the leader, to the molder, to the king of the masses. At the end of the mass movements of our time is the dictatorship.—Goebbels to Albrecht von Graefe, in *Die Zweite Revolution*, p. 16.

The Study of Factional Conflicts in German National Socialism

FEW aspects of the history of German National Socialism have received such scant scholarly attention as the nature of its factional conflicts. Although references to intraparty conflicts may be found in most accounts dealing with the movement, there has as yet been no attempt to make factional conflicts the subject of a thorough academic analysis.

Admittedly, factionalism was of only marginal significance in the history of the Nazi movement, and this may well account for the lagging academic interest in the subject. In striking contrast to socialist and communist movements, where factional conflicts have raised dramatic issues of theory leading frequently to a split in the party, Nazi factionalism was neither so dramatic nor so enduring in its effects. The several factions passed out of existence without seriously affecting the history of the Nazi movement. Factionalism did not split the movement, did not give rise to competing sets of leaders, did not seriously compromise Hitler's authority at any time, did not raise important theoretical questions, and, with the partial exception of 1934, did not result in mass purges within the party.

But the failure of Nazi factions can hardly justify the lack of interest in the subject. Indeed, it is exactly the impotence of the factions which should have raised some fundamental questions about the nature of factionalism in the movement. How, after all, can this impotence be explained in view of the considerable organizational strength and able leaders that these factions possessed? The Working Association of the

3

North and West in 1925–1926, the *Kampfverlag* circle in 1926–1930, and the Stormtroops (SA) until 1934 represented the most dynamic and powerful segments of the movement, yet when Hitler turned against them they dissolved almost instantly. Why did they not give rise to splinter movements? Why were the leaders of these factions, apparently so popular and powerful, abandoned by their followers at the crucial moment? Why were no mass purges necessary, and why were Hitler's authority and leadership never in serious jeopardy? Why, in short, was the experience with factional conflict in the Nazi party so radically different from that in the Marxist parties?

The fundamental proposition advanced here is that the nature or character of intragroup conflicts is intimately and directly related to the nature and character of the group itself. The nature of the group, that is, the nature of its cohesive forces, conditions the nature of the relations within the group and in turn the nature of internal conflicts and their resolution. Hence, differences in factional behavior are ultimately owing to differences in the nature of groups, specifically to differences in the focus of group cohesion. Accordingly, explanations for the peculiar patterns of Nazi factionalism have to be sought in the focus of group cohesions—or, in political terms, in the source of authority.

One of my purposes is to demonstrate the charismatic source of authority in the Nazi party. Hitler was the primary source of group cohesion, the focus of loyalty, and the personification of the utopian ideal —he was, in short, a charismatic leader. In contrast with Marxist parties, where ideology provides the highest source of authority, the Nazi party was based on charismatic legitimacy. The importance of this fundamental difference in the natures of the Nazi and the Marxist movements has been obscured by the "uni-totalitarian" approach, which, by concentrating on the common characteristics of totalitarian movements, has tended to neglect some significant peculiarities of these two movements (Groth, 1964; see Bibliography, pp. 153–158, for full description of references).

The source of authority, or the kind of legitimacy, is relevant to the nature of factionalism because, as the focus of group cohesion, it becomes the object, not the subject, of factional conflicts. Be it the charismatic leader or the ideology, the source of authority is the prize for which factions compete. The task of factions is to attain legitimacy by identifying themselves with the source of authority. Should a faction

4

fail in this endeavor, the members of the group will regard it as illegitimate, and it will either wither away for lack of support or split the movement and establish itself as an independent group. In either case, it will cease to be a faction.

Thus, the charismatic nature of legitimacy was of fundamental significance for the pattern of Nazi factionalism. Nazi factions did not organize against Hitler, but instead strove to the last minute of their existence to gain his support. Their objective was not to challenge Hitler's leadership, but to capture him for their respective points of view. As the source of authority, the leader could not be challenged, he could only be claimed. Consequently, Hitler remained above factional conflicts that took place on the secondary levels of leadership and thereby ensured the unity of the movement against the danger of factional splits. His role as the ultimate arbiter and the sole source of cohesion strengthened this power and continually enhanced his authority.

In contrast, in Marxist parties based on ideological authority, factions have usually appealed to the dogma for their legitimization. Leaders of communist and socialist parties have been historically involved in factional conflicts: they were the subjects, not the objects, of factional strife. The ideological source of authority raised factional disputes to the highest level of leadership and generated significant theoretical questions as all factions attempted to justify their positions by ideological orthodoxy. Factional conflicts in ideological movements constantly threatened their unity because these movements had no leader who could remain above the conflicts.

Although German Nazism came close to Max Weber's idea of charismatically legitimated authority, no studies have tested the empirical relevance and analytic utility of the concept of charisma in National Socialism. Some writers have given more attention to the significance of the concept for National Socialism than others (for example, Loewenstein, 1939; Neumann, 1944, pp. 83–97; Gerth, 1940), but it is safe to assert that "charisma" has been at best an incidental, rather than a primary concern in the literature on German Nazism. In most accounts, "charisma" has been used as a shorthand expression to indicate the importance of the demagogic, mesmerizing personality of Hitler, rather than as a concept to denote a special type of authority. The loose and undisciplined application of the term to anything from the predominant role of Hitler to the lack of philosophic content in National Socialism

5

has impaired the analytic usefulness of the concept and has raised serious questions about it (see especially Friedrich, 1961; Ratnam, 1964). Weber's concept of charismatic legitimacy will be my basic analytic tool in explaining the nature of Nazi factionalism. Specifically, this study will advance the proposition that the peculiar patterns of Nazi factionalism can be explained only by the charismatically legitimated authority in the Nazi party that conditioned the internal dynamics of the movement.

In Part One, I shall demonstrate the charismatic nature of legitimacy in the Nazi party by analyzing Hitler as a charismatic figure, the role of ideas in the movement, and the nature of party organization. Then I shall examine the relevance of charismatic legitimacy to the nature of factional conflicts, developing in the course of which a series of generalizations about the pattern of factionalism in the Nazi movement. In Part Two, these generalizations will be subjected to the test of historical data—basically, data about the two major factions that dominated the internal politics of the Nazi movement in its pre-power stage: the northern faction represented by Gregor and Otto Strasser, and the SA led by Ernst Röhm. The conclusion will present some ideas about the concept of factionalism in the hope that they may stimulate further studies on the subject.

卐 PART ONE

*CHARISMATIC LEGITIMACY
AND THE PATTERN OF FACTIONALISM*

I

Hitler as a Charismatic Leader

MAX WEBER's concept of charisma as a source of political authority rested on the axiom that every viable political order presumes "a certain minimum of voluntary submission . . . an interest in obedience" on the part of the subjects (Weber, 1947, p. 324). This consent to be ruled, or the recognition by subjects of their rulers' right to rule, denotes the value-free concept of legitimacy which may characterize such highly diverse forms of political orders as primitive societies, absolutist monarchies, and modern democracies. What differentiates these polities is not the presence or absence of legitimacy, but the nature of legitimacy. Historically, the right to rule (authority) has been accorded to rulers for different reasons depending on the prevalent political culture in the society. These reasons mark the bases of political obedience, or, in Weber's terms, the types of legitimacy.

Authority, according to Weber, may be legitimated traditionally, rational-legally, or charismatically. When subjects obey their rulers because of their "belief in the legitimacy of what has always existed," and when the rulers claim authority on the basis of "the sanctity of immemorial traditions," legitimacy is traditional. When subjects submit to their rulers because of "the legality of patterns of normative rulers," and when the rulers are recognized as rightful ones because their rule has been established in a legal manner, legitimacy is rational-legal. Finally, when subjects accord the right to rule to a person because of his "specific and exceptional sanctity, heroism or exemplary character," and when a person claims authority on the basis of his personal qualities and

9

his special mission, legitimacy is charismatic. (Weber, 1947, pp. 130, 328.)

It is outside the scope of this study to determine whether Weber's typology exhausts all possible bases of political obedience. One obvious difficulty with Weber's typology is that it does not recognize ideology as a source of authority. The object at hand, however, is not to suggest a new typology, but to examine the utility of the concept of charismatic authority for the analysis of German Nazism in general and of its factional conflicts in particular. The inadequacy of Weber's threefold classification of the bases of authority is irrelevant to the question whether charisma is a useful analytic tool.

The concept of charisma suggests several elements that can serve as basic points of reference for the analysis of National Socialism and that can, in turn, suggest a set of testable indices on the basis of which the charismatic nature of authority in National Socialism can be established. (For similar approaches, see Davies, 1954; Fagen, 1965.) Among the empirically significant elements of charismatic authority are: the existence of a person who is regarded by his followers as an individual of extraordinary powers or qualities; the notion of a utopian ideal in the form of a *Weltanschauung* whose realization becomes the mission of the charismatic leader; and the nonbureaucratic organization of the charismatically legitimated political order.[1] These elements suggest certain questions that may be posed for empirical analysis. Is there a person regarded by his followers as a man of "supernatural, superhuman, or at least specifically exceptional powers or qualities" by virtue of which he is empowered to create new obligations, to establish a new social order, in short, to rule in accordance with his conscience? (Weber, 1947, p. 358.) Is there a belief in a utopian ideal which serves as the ultimate justification of the political order and whose agent is the charismatic leader? Is the organization of the political order characterized primarily by "an emotional form of communal relationship" rather than by bureaucratic principles? (Weber, 1947, p. 360.) To answer these questions in the affirmative with respect to the German Nazi party is to demonstrate its charismatic character.

---

[1] The "routinization of charisma," although an important element in Weber's concept of charismatic authority, is omitted here because the subject of this study is not an established political order, but a political movement primarily in its pre-power stage.

A leader is charismatic if he is regarded by his followers as a person whose powers or qualities are so exceptional that they are of divine origin and inaccessible to the ordinary person. By virtue of such extraordinary, supernatural, or superhuman powers, the charismatic leader is permitted to rule. The actions of the charismatic leader can violate tradition as well as the legal framework; his legitimacy derives from his personal qualities, from his "gifts of grace" (Weber, 1947, p. 360). The significant aspect of charisma is that the extraordinary qualities of the leader are purely subjective, resting on the perception of his followers; they are not subject to any objective proof or verification. "Charisma" does not denote an objectively definable pattern of traits, nor does a charismatic leader need to satisfy any objective, ethical, aesthetic, or other criteria. "What alone is important," writes Weber, "is how an individual is actually regarded by those subject to charismatic authority, by his followers or disciples" (Weber, 1947, p. 359). Charisma, as Davies correctly points out, should not be considered as a "characteristic of leaders as such but [as] a relationship between leaders and followers" (1954, p. 1083).

Although charisma is subjective, resting on such qualities as the followers ascribe to the leader, it would be a mistake to assume that it could be ascribed to just anybody. There has to be a measure of extraordinariness in the person of the charismatic leader in order to evoke the enthusiasm and devotion necessary for the establishment of charismatic authority. What constitutes "extraordinariness" is of course again subjective, depending on the existing political culture, but it can hardly be doubted that a charismatic relation can be generated only by a person with some special qualities. Thus, no matter how extraordinary he may be, a person will not become a charismatic leader unless his extraordinariness is recognized by others. The transformation of extraordinariness into charisma depends on the political skills and magnetism of the potential charismatic leader and on his conviction of his historical role. A person, if he is successfully to transform extraordinariness into charisma, must take himself seriously; he must see himself as called to fulfill some historical mission. This sense of mission and its complements, the necessary political skills, are the prerequisites for the establishment of charismatic legitimacy.

11

Hitler took several years to transform his extraordinary personal qualities into charismatic authority in the Nazi party. According to Konrad Heiden (1935, p. 45), he began to take himself seriously only in the middle of the 1920's. It was in the second half of *Mein Kampf*, written after his release from prison, that he began to identify himself as the great man who "is the rarest thing to be found on this globe" (1939, p. 849). He saw himself as the messiah whose mission was to realize the "absolute idea" on earth. By 1930 he identified himself with the Weltanschauung (Strasser, *Ministersessel*, p. 17).

Concomitantly with his developing sense of mission, he was employing the necessary means to generate charismatic legitimacy. The greeting "Heil Hitler" (which, significantly, was used by Hitler himself), the elaborate ceremonies of mass meetings, and the oratory, demagogy, and rituals of the party festivities were all exploited to that end.

His fanatical belief in himself, his political skill in manipulating mass sentiment, and the large numbers of people who were looking for a leader and a cause enabled Hitler to become the focus of loyalty and the ultimate depository of authority in the movement by the late 1920's. He came to be obeyed by the majority of his party followers, and later by the majority of the nation, as a savior and a redeemer. Progressively, National Socialism became Hitlerism; its policies were Hitler's policies, its power was Hitler's power. By 1936 Hans Frank could be explicit about Hitler's charismatic authority: "There is in Germany today only one authority, and that is the authority of Führer" (1953, p. 137). The charismatic nature of authority found expression in Nazi jurisprudence, which was predicated on the slogan "Führerworte haben Gesetzes Kraft" (the words of the leader have the force of law); Hitler's orders, whether oral or written, canceled all written law.[2]

[2] See Hans Frank's "Directives for Judges," 1936; quoted in Blase, 1963, p. 78. Two paragraphs of this directive may be profitably quoted here:

"Grundlage der Auslegung aller Rechtsquellen ist die nationalsozialistische Weltanschauung wie sie insbesonderen in dem Parteiprogramm und den Äusserungen unseres Führers ihren Ausdruck findet.

"Gegenüber Führerentscheidungen, die in die Form eines Gesetztes oder einer Verordnung gekleidet sind, steht dem Richter kein Prüfungsrecht zu. Auch an sonstige Entscheidunges des Führers ist der Richter gebunden, sofern in ihnen der Wille, Recht zu setzen, unzweideutig zum Ausdruck kommt . . ."

Professor Carl Schmitt wrote in 1934 that "the real leader is always also a judge. Leadership is the source of judgeship." ("Der wahre Führer ist immer auch Richter. Aus dem Führertum fliesst das Richtertum.") Also quoted in Blase, 1963, p. 78.

Hitler's ability to evoke strong personal attachments was important in the creation of his charismatic authority. Some revered him as a godlike man,[3] and others followed him "with a passionate enthusiasm that beclouded all reason."[4] His personal influence was of such magnitude that when some old films were shown of him at Nuremberg after the war, "Ribbentrop was completely overwhelmed by the voice and figure of the Führer. He wept like a baby, as if a dead father had returned to life." "The Führer had a terrifically magnetic personality," Ribbentrop told Gilbert. "You can't understand it unless you've experienced it. Do you know, even now, six months after his death, I can't completely shake off his influence?" (Gilbert, 1961, pp. 61, 65). Ernst Kaltenbrunner reacted similarly to Hitler. "Hitler's personality held an almost mesmeric fascination for him; he sincerely worshipped him and he had an unbounded faith in what he regarded as his inspired foresight and vision" (Hoettl, 1954, p. 66).

Hitler emerges from Joseph Goebbels's early secret diary as an extraordinary figure with whom Goebbels completely identified. His trusts and distrusts, pleasures and displeasures, presence and absence affected Goebbels deeply and intimately. He was hurt when he thought he had lost Hitler's confidence and exulted when he enjoyed his support. When in 1926 he found himself at odds with Hitler, he was crushed: "My heart aches so much . . . I have been deprived of my inner self. I am only half." When Hitler later invited him to Munich, Goebbels was as elated as a child: "I am born again . . . I am a man again . . . I am happy." And some weeks later: "I feel myself bound again at last. My last doubts are gone. *Heil Hitler.*" Goebbels loved Hitler, felt small beside him, and could not bear to be disappointed by him: "Adolf Hitler I love you, because you are great and pure at the same time."[5]

Hitler's personality was felt not only by his immediate subordinates, but also by the mass of his followers. His capacity to make people follow him in blind fanaticism, to bring them under his spell, has been recounted by many eyewitnesses. Putzi Hanfstängl, one of Hitler's confidants, described the audience at a meeting in 1922: "I looked at the audience. Where was the nondescript crowd I had seen only an hour be-

[3] Robert Ley, for instance, according to Kelley, 1947, p. 156.
[4] Hans Frank to Gilbert, in Gilbert, 1961, p. 137.
[5] Heiber, n.d., pp. 33–34, 43, 60, 68, 74, 94 (October 12, 1925, to April 19, 1926). It is significant to note that Goebbels did not write this diary for later publication.

fore? What was suddenly holding these people . . . ? The hubbub and the mugclattering had stopped and they were drinking in every word. Only a few yards away was a young woman, her eyes fastened on the speaker. Transfixed as though in some devotional ecstasy, she had ceased to be herself and was completely under the spell of Hitler's despotic faith in Germany's future greatness" (Hanfstängl, 1957, p. 35).

William L. Shirer rendered a similar account twelve years later about the Nuremberg party rally: "About ten o'clock tonight I got caught in a mob of ten thousand hysterics who jammed the moat in front of Hitler's hotel, shouting: 'We want our Führer.' I was a little shocked at the faces, especially those of the women, when Hitler finally appeared on the balcony for a moment. They reminded me of the crazed expressions I saw once in the back country of Louisiana on the faces of some Holy Rollers who were about to hit the trail. They looked up at him as if he were a Messiah, their faces transformed into something positively inhuman" (1961, p. 17).

There can be little doubt that what attracted most people to National Socialism was Hitler, who could express the aspirations as well as the frustrations and the resentments of the masses. Kurt Lüdecke, a former Nazi and an acute observer of National Socialism, related his first encounter with Hitler. At that moment he knew that his long search was ended: "I had found myself, my leader and my cause . . . I had given him my soul" (1938, pp. 23–25). Goebbels reacted similarly: "From this moment I am born again, I am intoxicated" (in Bramstedt, 1954, p. 68). "It is impossible to describe the experience of seeing and hearing the leader for the first time," wrote one of Theodore Abel's respondents in 1934. "One thing is certain: from that day on I had no other purpose than to fight for him until victory was won" (Abel, 1938, p. 214). "In July the leader came to Tilsit," wrote another. "I saw him for the first time . . . Those hours are never to be forgotten. The leader spoke. For the first time I heard his voice. His words went straight to the heart. From now on my life and efforts were dedicated to the leader. I wanted to be a true follower" (Abel, 1938, p. 298).

Further examples would only belabor the point that Hitler's followers regarded him as more than an ordinary leader (cf. Gisevius, 1963, pp. 65, 105, and *passim*; Glum, 1962, p. 122; Lüdecke, 1938, p. 344 and *passim*). Even such a cynical member of his inner circle as Göring admitted as much after the war (Gilbert, 1961, p. 341). It is not an exag-

14

geration to conclude from the depositions and memoirs of Nazi followers that for them Hitler was a *homo novus,* a person of extraordinary
gifts beyond ordinary men. He possessed the confidence of the masses
who "surrendered to him with hysterical enthusiasm . . . and followed
him with a mad jubilation" (as Hans Frank told Gilbert, 1961, p. 137).
He was the tribune of the people, possessing their souls and giving their
life a new meaning.[6] There is little doubt that for the majority of his followers he was the movement and the idea—in short, he was the source
of legitimacy.

[6] The dramatic statement illustrating this point was Göring's. In the early 1930's
he told Hermann Rauschning; "I have no conscience. Adolf Hitler is my conscience"
(Rauschning, 1940, p. 77). See also Abel, 1938, pp. 138, 146, 151–154; Springer,
1949, p. 160; Jarman, 1956, p. 153; Lüdecke, 1938, p. 340.

II

The Role of Ideas in the Nazi Movement

ONE aspect of charismatic authority has been frequently neglected: the belief in some higher power or ultimate ideal is just as essential to charismatic legitimacy as is a person capable of generating popular enthusiasm and fanatical devotion.[1] Although the charismatic leader is the creation of his followers who accord him the right to rule because of his extraordinary powers or qualities, both leader and followers are enthralled by the myth of a higher mission. The leader's "gifts of grace," by virtue of which he is recognized as a charismatic person, are thought to derive from a higher source, and the qualities attributed to him are considered the manifestations of the mission that he has been called to fulfill.[2]

Thus, the charismatic leader is the agent not of his disciples, but of a higher power or idea. As a political leader he is the tribune of the people, who provide the source of his political power but not of his legitimacy; charismatic authority does not recognize the concept of popular sovereignty. The charismatic leader is responsible to his conscience alone and, transcendentally, to the source of his legitimacy—be that God,

[1] Shils (1965, p. 201) writes: "The charismatic quality of an individual as perceived by others, or himself, lies in what is thought to be his connection with (including possession by or embodiment of) some very central feature of man's existence and the cosmos in which he lives." See also Weber, 1947, p. 360; Fagen, 1965, pp. 275–284.

[2] "We know that we all stood under this command of Fate," said Hitler on the anniversary of the abortive revolt of November, 1923, "that we were assuredly but the instruments of a Higher Power." (Baynes, 1942, Vol. I, p. 150). The significance of the coronation ceremonies of the Capetian kings provides an interesting example of the relation of charisma and a higher power. See Maurois, 1960, p. 41, and Loewenstein, 1939, pp. 29–32.

16

History, or Nature. He is responsive to the masses because he is dependent on their support, but he is responsible only to his conscience because he is the agent of a higher power. He is the leader of the masses, not their agent.[3]

Although, as Carl J. Friedrich has pointed out, a belief in God was notoriously lacking in Nazism,[4] National Socialists were imbued with a sense of mission bordering on the religious. Hitler pictured himself and was regarded by his followers as the agent of "a general spiritual conception" which was the foundation of the future. He was the man who, having gained insight into the "absolute truth," was called upon to transmit this truth to the rest of mankind. He was chosen by Destiny to fulfill the great mission which "the Creator of the Universe" allotted to him. He was the spiritual founder, the prophet of the new doctrine, the "polar star" of the new order, the personification of the Weltanschauung. (Hitler, 1939, pp. 284, 481, 575–576, 752.)

Although the substance and reality of the Nazi "spiritual conception" is of as little consequence here as Hitler's insight into the nature of the "absolute truth," the mere existence of such beliefs indicates the importance of ideas in charismatically legitimated authority. The special relation of the leader and the Weltanschauung provided the basis of the National Socialist "leader-principle" (*Führerprinzip*), which denoted the absolute, all-embracing authority of the leader in the movement. As the person with the unique insight into the absolute truth, Hitler could claim for himself a position which generated an aura of mystery around his person. This and his undoubted personal magnetism and oratorical power helped to establish his charismatic authority. The relative importance of the Weltanschauung and his special abilities in the establishment of charismatic legitimacy is problematical, but the success of their combination is a matter of historical record.

The National Socialist Weltanschauung (or, the National Socialist Idea) has been dismissed by many scholars on grounds that it was too

---

[3] The dual aspect of charismatic leadership was recognized by Hitler. He acknowledged his popular source of power when he told the people that "Everything that I am I am through you . . ." but he rejected the idea of responsibility to them in his talk with Otto Strasser. (*Trial*, 1947–1949, Vol. XXIX, Doc. 2168-PS, pp. 279–308; Strasser, *Ministersessel*, p. 17.)

[4] This has been one of his reasons for disputing the charismatic nature of the Nazi movement (1961, pp. 3–24). For other critiques of the notion of charisma in general and the charismatic character of the Hitler movement in particular see Ratnam, 1964, pp. 341–354; Friedrich and Brzezinski, 1965, pp. 41–42.

vague to be meaningful, too contradictory to make philosophic or scientific sense, and too demagogic to be anything but propaganda in Hitler's hands. Many observers have agreed with Franz Neumann's conclusion that Nazism had no political or social theory, no philosophy, and no concern for the truth (1944, pp. 437–438). "Hitlerism," wrote Claude David, "was not a doctrine, it was a movement. It had an ideology only to give orientation to its propaganda" (1954, p. 37). Or, in the catch phrase of Zevedei Barbu, Hitlerism was "a mystique for action," whose ideology was but a futile attempt to conceal its naked will to power (Barbu, 1956, p. 136; see also Broszat, 1958, p. 53; Greenwood, 1934, p. 8; Baumont *et al.*, 1955, p. 481).

Such views of the role of the National Socialist Idea have been stated by leading Nazis themselves. Heinrich Himmler is reported to have expressed contempt for "ideological phantasies," and Hermann Göring declared after the war that he joined the movement because it was revolutionary, not because of the "ideological stuff" (Kersten, 1952, p. 26; Kelley, 1947, p. 64). Hermann Rauschning thought that the distinguishing feature of Nazism was not a different ideology, but the total lack of one (1938, pp. 39–41, 88). Several Nazi leaders held the Nazi program of 1920 in contempt and dismissed its significance for the success of the movement. Joseph Goebbels is reported to have declared that if he had founded the party, he would not have drawn up a program at all.[5] Julius Streicher testified at Nuremberg that for him the program was superfluous. "I admit frankly," he said, "that I never read it in its entirety" (*Trials*, Vol. XII, p. 344). This opinion was shared by Hans Fritzsche, who wrote shortly after the war that "the National Socialist Party got the least number of its members through its Program" (Springer, 1949, p. 157).

In view of such widespread opinion, it appears strange that the "Idea," alternatively called the "Weltanschauung," "Fundamental Principle," or "Absolute Truth," should have played such a prominent role in National Socialist propaganda. Yet it is difficult to find a speech by Hitler or any other leading Nazi that does not refer to the historic importance of "fundamental views of life." The Nazis believed all great historic changes had been the manifestations of great ideas. Without ideas only

[5] *Vossische Zeitung*, July, 1934, No. 158. "I wish to God," Konrad Heiden quotes Goebbels saying, "we had never heard of those miserable twenty-five points" (Heiden, 1944, p. 40).

governments can be changed, not political and social systems.[6] "All force," wrote Goebbels in the same spirit, "which does not spring from a firm spiritual foundation will be hesitating and uncertain. It will lack stability which can only be based on a fanatical view of life" (1937, p. 222).

Thus, the student of German Nazism is confronted with two apparently irreconcilable positions. On the one hand, the majority of scholarly opinion has dismissed the ubiquity of the Nazi Weltanschauung and has interpreted Nazism as an opportunistic, action-oriented movement interested solely in gaining political power. On the other hand, the ubiquitous Weltanschauung in Nazi speeches and other documents makes it difficult to regard this as mere rhetoric. Nazi sources convey a compelling impression that they indeed believe in the "eternal values of blood and soil" and that the Weltanschauung both constituted an important part of Nazi appeals and was indispensable to Hitler's charisma.[7]

The key to the solution of this dilemma lies in the separation of the concept of ideology from the Nazi notion of Weltanschauung. Although Nazi spokesmen carefully avoided the term, scholars, especially in the Anglo-Saxon world, have persistently translated Weltanschauung as "ideology." Unfortunately, however, despite some similarities, the two concepts are not only too distinct to be identified without doing injustice to both of them, but also, most important for this study, whereas one is compatible with charismatic authority, the other is not.

Weltanschauung and ideology are similar in that they both attempt to apply general ideas to specific situations and thereby attempt to establish explicit moral bases for action (Apter, 1964, pp. 16–17). They both present value judgments as empirical truths in order to justify a particular group's claim to social and political dominance (Metzger, 1949, p. 125). They both claim perennial insights to justify political action (Germino, 1963, p. 448). They both attempt to provide "more than purely rational satisfactions from political activity"; and they both attempt to render otherwise meaningless situations meaningful (Apter, 1964, p. 29; Geertz, in *ibid.*, p. 64).

[6] Hitler's speech of February 24, 1934, in Baynes, 1942, Vol. I, p. 145; also his speech of March 19, 1934, *ibid.*, p. 211.

[7] Aside from Nazi sources, this point of view is supported by Hajo Holborn, who described Hitler as "a doctrinaire of the first order," and ascribed a continuous and consistent role to Nazi ideas in the movement, which, in his view, represented more than a mere instrumentality for gaining power (Holborn, 1964).

However, the crucial point of difference between Weltanschauung and ideology is that, whereas the former is confined to remote and abstract ideas, the latter comprises both the ultimate goal and the political program necessary for its realization. A Weltanschauung is an esoteric notion belonging to the "metaphysically unlimited world of thought"; it is meaningful only to philosophers and saints (Hitler, 1939, p. 574). Ideology, on the other hand, "is not merely a statement of ends, but an instrument for achieving these ends" (Wirth, 1940, p. 480). A Weltanschauung consists of vague and "unshaped material"; an ideology is a "brief system . . . a configuration of ideas and attitudes in which the elements are bound together by some form of constraint of functional interdependence" (Hitler, 1939, p. 583; Converse, in Apter, 1964, p. 207).

Thus, ideology is the logic or science of ideas, and Weltanschauung denotes only an idea (or ideas). In political parlance, ideology consists of a purpose or a series of political principles *and* of a program of political action, but a Weltanschauung is confined to principles of importance for centuries. In the words of C. Wendell King, the minimum function of an ideology "is to provide a rationale not only for the objectives but for the tactical and organizational means to those objectives—it must make a good case for what the movement is trying to do and how it is trying to do it" (1956, pp. 69–70). Hence, an ideology is an "action-related" system of ideas or "a system of ideas set up for the sake of action,"[8] whereas a Weltanschauung does not necessarily imply political action but can merely represent the discovery of some principle or truth. "Ideology" is a political concept, but Weltanschauung may transcend the limits of the political to encompass the moral, aesthetic, and social spheres of life.[9]

The significant difference between the two is that Weltanschauung is indispensable to charismatic authority and ideology is incompatible with

[8] Germino, p. 498. Ideology is "a consistent and integrated pattern of thoughts and beliefs explaining man's attitude towards life and his existence in society, and advocating a conduct of action pattern responsive to and commensurate with such thoughts and beliefs" (Loewenstein, 1953, pp. 52–53). Cf. Daniel Bell's definition: "Ideology is a conversion of ideas into social levels" (1961, p. 394).

[9] Apter, 1964, p. 17. "The National Socialist revolution encompasses the whole life," wrote Alfred Rosenberg in his diary. "It influences character, inner values, and the soul. It reforms the whole man" (Seraphim, 1956, pp. 148ff). Goebbels wrote in the same vein: "The Nazi revolution represented the transvaluation of all values and the overthrow of a value system [Gedankenwelt]" (1937, p. 7).

it. A charismatic leader may consider himself to be the instrument of an abstract ideal without impairing his charismatic legitimacy, but he cannot consider himself to be the agent of an ideology, which always represents some measure of constraint that a charismatic leader of absolute authority cannot accept. A chiliastic idea is infinitely malleable—it can be what the leader says it is. Charismatic authority and ideology are incompatible also because both can serve the function of organizing political support for some ideal goal. An ideology attracts adherents by its goal and its program, thereby becoming a focus of loyalty and a source of legitimacy. A charismatic leader attracts adherents to the extent that he succeeds in incorporating the utopian goal in his person. Thus, ideology and charismatic leadership fulfill the same function of translating the ideal principle or purpose into a political program, and in this sense they represent alternative sources of authority rather than complementary forces. Ideologies do not have prophets—utopian ideas do.

This crucial difference between ideology and Weltanschauung manifests itself in the role of the leader. In an ideological movement, the leader is merely the spokesman for the ideology, which expresses the ultimate ideas as well as the program of the movement; the leader claims authority on the basis of the ideology, the source of legitimacy. Thus, regardless of how absolute their power may be, leaders of ideologically legitimated movements are always careful to justify their power ideologically and to appear mere instruments of the ideology. Such leaders continually face the problem of the "cult of personality," a charismatic type of legitimacy.

The role of the leader in a movement based on a "fundamental view of life" is essentially different because a Weltanschauung is restricted to the esoteric realm. Unlike the Marxist ideology, the Nazi Weltanschauung was a meaningless abstraction until it was personified in Hitler. "An idea needs somebody to represent it," wrote Rosenberg; "man, idea and work form an inseparable unity" (1932, p. 7). The role of the charismatic leader is not merely to serve as a spokesman for an already defined ideology, but to forge "out of the purely metaphysically unlimited world of thought a clearly outlined faith" (Hitler, 1939, p. 574). The charismatic leader is not the interpreter of an ideology, but the discoverer of an idea. In Hitler's words, "An ingenious idea originates in the brains of a man who now feels himself called upon to transmit his knowledge to the rest of mankind" (1939, p. 481). The charismatic

21

leader defines the "general spiritual conception" and formulates a program that becomes "the banner of a fighting movement."[10]

Two aspects of the relation of leader and idea in a charismatically legitimated movement deserve special emphasis. One is their inseparability. The term "leader" implies by definition the personification of a Weltanschauung. A Weltanschauung, in turn, is created by a man of spiritual force and imagination who has been chosen by Destiny to bring it down to earth.[11] A Weltanschauung is not so much an objective entity or a logical construct, but the subjective experience of a man who believes himself called upon to transmit this spiritual conception to the rest of mankind (Hitler, 1939, p. 481). In this manner the complete identification of the leader and the idea is achieved. Hitler strongly implied this in *Mein Kampf* and explicitly stated it in 1930 (Strasser, *Ministersessel*, p. 9). As a result of this identification, no legitimate questions can be raised about the leader's conception or interpretation of the idea. The idea has to be what the leader says it is; the moment this assumption is not accepted, he ceases to be the leader. Thus, legitimacy resides in the leader, who, for all practical purposes, is the idea.

The other aspect of the relation of leader and idea is the necessity for distinguishing between the program and the Weltanschauung. The Weltanschauung is a utopian idea representing the ultimate goal of the movement, whereas the program is an opportunistic instrument in the hands of the leader. The Weltanschauung is a philosophic, religious reflection of the absolute truth; the program is a political instrument adjusted to the psychology of the masses.

The need for a program stems from the recognition that the Weltanschauung will be realized only if the masses are willing to fight for it. "Every view of life," wrote Hitler, "though it may be right a thousand times and of the highest value to mankind, will remain without importance . . . unless its principles have become the banner of a fighting

---

[10] Hitler, 1939, p. 575. Cf. Sukarno's Marhaenism of which he designated himself "The Custodian": "Marhaenism is the formulation and reflection of the ideals, ideas, thoughts, and emotions as to State and Society that *potentially* slumber in the minds and hearts of the Marhaen-masses who are unable to express these things for themselves. Understanding the *unvoiced ideals* of these masses, the Marhaenists long ago embarked upon the task of translating and formulating those ideals into Marhaenism and of guiding them and fighting alongside them for its realization." (The Manifesto of Marhaenism, quoted in Hanna, 1964, p. 14.)

[11] Hitler, 1939, pp. 394, 752. Sometimes Hitler talks about the leader as the discoverer of the idea, at other times, its creator.

movement . . ." (Hitler, 1939, p. 575). However, the metaphysical idea of the Weltanschauung is too vague to imbue the masses with the enthusiasm necessary for revolutionary action. Hitler was convinced that the receptive ability of the masses is limited, their understanding small, and their forgetfulness great. They are motivated not by reason, but by feeling and sentiment; they are primitive, driven by hysteria, and capable only of religious fanaticism. Hitler said masses have the feminine characteristic of despising vague ideas and objective viewpoints; they are animated by fanatically one-sided orientations and are attracted by power and strength (1939, pp. 234, 467–468; Rauschning, 1940, p. 177).

The Weltanschauung in its pure form is incapable of mobilizing the masses, not only because of its esoteric nature but also because its goal is too remote and too intangible to appeal to the masses, who are attracted by proximate goals and concrete promises. "The whole mass of workers," Hitler is reported to have said in 1930, "wants nothing else than bread and games; they have no understanding for any ideals" (Heiden, 1944, p. 59). Hence, the program is necessary. "Out of general conceptions a political program, and out of a general view of life a definite political program, and out of a general view of life a definite political faith have to be coined" in order to mobilize the masses for action (Hitler, 1939, p. 576). The program is therefore a political instrument concerned not with the absolute truth, but with definite political goals. Unlike the Weltanschauung, it is not to be judged by any absolute standard, but simply by its success in organizing mass support for the Weltanschauung.[12]

The gap between the masses and the Weltanschauung not only makes the program necessary, but also suggests the historic task of the extraordinary leader who formulates the program and brings the Weltanschauung to the level of the masses in the form of a fanatical faith. Such a person, according to Hitler, has to be a psychologist and a politician. He has to understand the psyche of the masses in order to be their recognized leader. He has to be a man who can transmit the "wavering and infinitely interpretable purely spiritual idea" to the masses. But, if he is to be a revolutionary leader instead of a mere politician, he has to be also a philosopher who understands the ab-

[12] Hitler is clearly contradictory when he alternatively refers to the Weltanschauung as a purely subjective idea and as a conception which can be judged by absolute standards.

23

solute idea. This capacity for being simultaneously a philosopher and a politician is a truly rare phenomenon, the mark of an extraordinary man. "The combination of theorist, organizer, and leader in one person is the rarest thing to be found on this globe; this combination makes the great man" (Hitler, 1939, p. 849). The leader as the philosopher and the psychologist conveys the notion of an extraordinary figure who is at the same time the prophet of the Weltanschauung and the tribune of the people. As a philosopher, his thought is governed by the eternal truth, and his greatness is founded on the absolute and abstract correctness of his idea; as a politician, he is concerned with the realizable political goal, and his greatness depends on his success as an organizer. As a philosopher, he is removed from this world into the realm of metaphysics; as a politician, he is a man of action concerned with the problems of the day. As a philosopher, his importance lies in the future: the gods like him if he asks for the impossible; as a politician, his concerns relate to practical goals and accomplishments. As a philosopher, he is the only one who "has full insight into, and exact knowledge of the ultimate ideas" (Hitler, 1939, p. 678); as a politician, he is the only man who expresses the will of the people (Loewenstein, 1939, p. 46).

The difference between the Weltanschauung and the program in Nazi thought not only is crucial to the Nazi concept of leadership (Führerprinzip) but also casts light on the controversies that surrounded the program in the 1920's. When, after 1925, the northerners suggested revision of the program of 1920, Hitler refused and declared the program unalterable.[13] He did so not because he believed the program to represent the essence of National Socialism, but because he considered it dangerous to alter it. He said repeatedly that what the masses want is faith, not truth. One cannot have faith in something that is changing. Since the program should be evaluated not by the Weltanschauung but solely by political efficacy, its substance should not be debated. The program is not for the elite, but for the masses (Bullock, 1959, p. 68). It has to create fanatical believers by giving them something concrete and unalterable. If it succeeds in this, it is right, regardless of the correctness of its specific formulation.

Thus, the people who argued about the substance of the program failed to understand its basic function and met with Hitler's contempt.

[13] See the Constitution of the NSDAP, May 22, 1926 (Stanford University, *Documents*, Reel 3, Folder 79. Also Hitler, 1953, p. 184).

Some of the original founders of the party, Anton Drexler and Gottfried Feder among them, argued about the program, and when Hitler disregarded their suggestions, they were disappointed and felt betrayed (Rauschning, 1938, p. 38). But it was they who were wrong. They did not understand the nature of politics in the age of the masses or realize what Hitler realized well—that it is not to intellect and substance, but to emotions and symbolism, that a mass leader has to address himself.

The program of 1920 was a symbolic rather than a substantive representation of the National Socialist Idea. The Nazi elite could deal with it contemptuously since it was not designed for them. A program of substantive goals would have limited Hitler's opportunistic course and, more important, would have been incompatible with his concept of absolute leadership. Even as it was, the program occasionally embarrassed Hitler, yet he never repudiated it because he would have had to replace it with another. Thus, neither National Socialism nor Hitler were to be tied by the program.[14]

The manifestation of ideas in the Nazi party in the form of the Weltanschauung provides another indication of the importance of charismatic leadership in the movement. The Weltanschauung provided the utopian goal ultimately justifying the movement—which, however, remained so remote and undefined that it needed an interpreter, a prophet to bring it down to the masses. The person who could claim successfully to have direct and exclusive access to the absolute truth was increasingly regarded by his followers as extraordinary. Hence, the Weltanschauung of the Nazi movement enabled Hitler to claim charismatic authority with increasing success after his initial appearance in politics. Although his personal magnetism and oratorical talents were indispensable to the establishment of his charisma, they were merely necessary means to convey the idea of his mission as the agent of the utopian idea. The Weltanschauung provided the positive aspect of Nazi appeals, albeit remote and vague. One might suggest that it supplied the substance and Hitler's oratory and magnetism supplied the form—in this sense, they complemented each other; Hitler's success in becoming a charismatic leader was predicated on their fortuitous combination.

[14] *Mein Kampf* came dangerously close to being an ideological statement of Nazi principles and objectives. According to Frank, Hitler regretted ever having written it, and allowed nobody to quote from it without his permission (Frank, 1953, pp. 45–46; see also Wendt, 1933, p. 23).

III

The Nature of Party Organization

ACCORDING to Weber, charismatically legitimated groups are based on an "emotional form of communal relationship" rather than on such bureaucratic principles as impersonality, hierarchy, and formal rules (1947, p. 360). Instead of officials selected for competence, the charismatic leader has disciples whom he selects for private reasons. The organization is predicated on the absolute and arbitrary authority of the leader, who obeys the call of a higher power rather than a system of formal rules. "Charismatic authority is thus specifically outside the realm of everyday routine," wrote Weber, "and . . . is sharply opposed both to rational, and particularly bureaucratic authority . . ." (1947, pp. 363–364). Overlapping spheres of competence, private relations, and the lack of any clear-cut hierarchy of officials characterize charismatically legitimated groups. The subordinates of the leader are chosen on personal grounds and partake of the leader's charisma as his representatives.

The peculiar characteristics of the Nazi party organization that, according to Hitler, none of the other parties possessed (1939, p. 857), have to be seen in the context of two major functions which the organization was to fulfill. Its explicit and obvious role was to serve as Hitler's instrument, to help him to "transmit his knowledge to the rest of mankind" and to reorganize society on the basis of the Weltanschauung (Hitler, 1939, pp. 481, 848; Görlitz & Quint, 1952, p. 159). The implicit and perhaps more significant function which conditioned the organizational principles of the party was to generate, maintain, and enhance Hitler's charismatic authority.

The purely instrumental role of the party and its auxiliary bodies was explicitly stated in *Mein Kampf* (p. 481) and repeatedly stressed by subsequent official and unofficial statements. The SA order of 1926, for instance, stated that the "S.A. is a means to an end," the end being the victory of the Weltanschauung (National Archives, *German Documents*, Reel 85). Hitler as the voice of the Weltanschauung had absolute power over the organization. He recognized no rules and considered the party and its formations his personal instruments. He could and did demote or promote not only persons but whole segments of the movement—as the radically changing positions of the SA, SS, and SD illustrated in the course of its history (Arendt, 1958, pp. 367, 400). The most dramatic expression of the purely instrumental role of the party was given by Hitler at an informal gathering after the party rally of 1938. He told his companions that if he ever came to the conclusion that the party was unnecessary for the historical task posed for him, he would not hesitate to destroy it (Frank, 1953, pp. 235–236).

Hitler's aversion to rules and his insistence on the unconditional authority of his will precluded the organization of the party on bureaucratic principles. Hierarchy, explicit and impersonal systems of rules, security of tenure, merit systems, and the bureaucratic values of competence and efficiency were anathema to him because he saw in them a limitation of his authority. He correctly recognized that any bureaucratic order, no matter how authoritarian it may be, limits arbitrary power and gives some protection to the subject and the underling administrator. For this reason Hitler was opposed to the issuance of codes and even refused to give legal forms to such important National Socialist projects as the Workers Front or the euthanasia program (Buchheim *et al.*, 1960, p. 11).

Hitler admitted his blatant disregard for party bylaws and procedures with considerable pride. During 1919–1920 the party organization followed the rules prescribed by German law for political parties. The leadership was elected by party meetings, and the party chairman was selected annually by a general conference. The party bylaws provided for committee meetings where minutes were kept and decisions were made by majority rule (Hitler, 1939, pp. 857–858; Jarman, 1956, p. 126; Dietrich, 1955, p. 141). When he took over the party chairmanship in August, 1921, Hitler did away with all this "lunacy." Although he had to keep up the façade to retain the legal status of the party, he rapidly emasculated the formal institutions and procedures (Hitler, 1939, pp. 866–867, and 1953, p. 230). The party rallies that grew out of the annual meetings of delegates became purely symbolic affairs; their function was neither to hammer out conflicting positions nor to "clarify unripe and uncertain ideas," but merely to serve as occasions "which once a year should unite the whole movement."[1]

In place of the formal procedures for making decisions, Hitler introduced the principle of "absolute authority and freedom towards below and duty and complete obediency towards above" (1939, p. 867)— which meant, above all, that the leader had unrestricted authority over the whole movement. He was not subject to any controls in the form of requirements for a majority, procedural rules, or lines of authority. He could exercise his authority in any manner he chose, or he could delegate any portion of it to whomever he chose. His authority was arbitrary, derived not from any institution but from his person, in accordance with the indivisible nature of charismatic authority: both in theory and in practice only one authority was decisive in the movement, and that was the will of the leader (Czech-Jochberg, 1933, p. 30). In the words of Hans Frank, Hitler's was a "purely personal rule resting on the Führer's will which was not to be hindered, influenced or advised by party program or anything else" (1953, p. 336).

As the sole source of authority, Hitler could delegate power in an arbitrary, highly personal manner (Dietrich, 1955, pp. 189–190). He distributed offices and assigned commissions on the basis of his trust and confidence, with the result that the members of the inner circle of the Nazi elite—that is, those who were commissioned directly by Hitler —were not "subject to any rule other than to the changing personality preferences of the leader" (Gerth, 1940, p. 521). Power and authority delegated by Hitler were rarely specified, and specific offices and commissions did not have clearly outlined competences; rather, the authority of the subleader depended on the extent to which he possessed Hitler's confidence (Gerth, 1940, p. 520). According to Hoettl,[2] Himm-

---

[1] Hitler's speech at the 1926 party rally, Baynes, 1942, Vol. I, p. 196. After 1937 no gauleiter or cabinet meetings were held (Fest, 1963, p. 70).

[2] Hoettl, 1954, p. 47. Hitler and other leading Nazis constantly emphasized the importance of personality and character in the selection of subordinates. See Goebbels, 1937, pp. 16–17; Hitler, 1953, p. 432.

ler's most important position was his relation to Hitler. The relation of Hitler to his subleaders has been aptly compared to that of the medieval overlord to his vassals-in-chief, who were bound to him by personal oaths.[3]

Hitler's disbursement of offices made for great insecurity among his subordinates. Having no bureaucratic rules to protect them, they were at Hitler's mercy and had to compete constantly for his favors. If, as Germino has suggested (1958, p. 4), the task of modern totalitarian movements is to keep the masses continually wedded to their cause, the organizational principles of the Nazi party were successful because they kept subleaders continually wedded to Hitler. A singularly striking case of such dependence was revealed by Felix Kersten. When in June, 1944, he suggested to Himmler that he should disregard certain orders from Hitler about the Jews, Himmler said that Hitler would never forgive him and would have him hanged immediately. Kersten looked at him in astonishment and asked whether his position were really as weak as all that (1952, pp. 162–163). Rauschning and Hjalmar Schacht reported in their memoirs similar dependence by district leaders and party officials (Rauschning, 1940, pp. 203–204; Trial, Doc. 3936-PS, Vol. XXXIII, pp. 559–563).

The competition for Hitler's favors resulted in bitter feuds, shifting alliances, and radical changes of power among the members of the Nazi elite. During 1925 Rosenberg feuded with Max Amann on the one hand, and with Esser and Hanfstängl on the other. In 1926 angry disputes broke out between Koch and Goebbels, Streicher and Esser, and Koch and Kaufmann. The animosities between the Munich group and the northerners spanned the years from 1924 to the early 1930's. The alliances and counteralliances among the members of the Nazi elite changed continually. In 1934 Himmler, Heydrich, Bürchel, Goebbels, and Papen made common cause against Röhm and Göring, and Goebbels and Hassel fought Rosenberg's influence. The maze of alliances at times verged on the comical. In the late 1920's, for instance, his opposition to the Strasser brothers induced Goebbels to befriend Pfeffer only because the latter was also the Strassers' enemy. Goebbels and Kauf-

---

[3] Neumann, 1965, p. 80. See, for instance, the wording of the SS oath: "I swear to you, Adolf Hitler, as Führer and Chancellor of the Reich, fidelity and bravery. I promise you and to those superiors appointed by you, obedience unto death, so help me God" (Trial, Doc. PS-3429, Vol. XXXII, p. 284).

mann were enemies, which made Terboven, who was Kaufmann's enemy, Goebbels's friend.[4]

The fortunes of party leaders depended entirely on Hitler's attitude. The decline of Feder after 1923 and of Rosenberg after 1932 as well as the rise of Goebbels, Göring, and Himmler can be directly attributed to Hitler's changing attitudes toward these people (Lüdecke, 1938, p. 457). The intrigues, alliances, and constant jockeying for position that characterized the internal relations of the Nazi elite all reflected the insecurity of their positions' resting not on established rules, but on the personal whims of the leader.

The personal disbursement of offices and the principle of "absolute authority and freedom towards below and duty and complete obedience towards above" was applied not only at the top of the Nazi hierarchy but also at secondary levels. The district leaders (gauleiters), as well as those responsible for the various auxiliary party organizations, were given the "widest possible powers of self government," which meant that they had private domains (Hitler, 1953, p. 433). Hitler's leadership principle was followed by his subordinates, who, within their spheres of competence, exercised their authority in strikingly similar patterns and established relations with their subordinates similar to those Hitler established in the movement as a whole. Their domains were regarded as their possessions, over which their authority was unlimited—subject to no limitation except the ultimate authority of the Führer.[5] As a result of their immense powers, many district leaders, assured of Hitler's confidence and support, began to behave like little Hitlers and "acquired a godlike semblance in their sphere and did what they pleased" (National Archives, *German Documents*, Reel 85).

The delegation of domains is inherent in the charismatic nature of authority, which can be bestowed on disciples but cannot be parceled. Local leaders claimed to be the personal representatives of Hitler and

[4] No systematic study has been made of these rivalries and alliances, but references to them can be found in almost every memoir or study dealing with National Socialism. The examples above have been taken from the following sources: Lüdecke, 1938, pp. 248–250, 256–266; Rosenberg, 1955, p. 190; Orb, 1945, p. 131; Heiden, 1944, pp. 290–293; Seraphim, 1956, p. 18; Kelley, 1947, p. 65; Miltenberg, 1931, p. 23; Hale, 1958, p. 358.

[5] The private character of the delegated domains was illustrated by Ribbentrop's note to Himmler expressing joy over his appointment as Obergruppenführer of the SS: "You know how I think of *your* SS," he wrote (italics mine) (*Trial*, Doc. 512, Vol. XXXIX, pp. 553–554; also Kersten, 1952, p. 261). Hitler often referred to the SA as "my SA" (Rauschning, 1940, p. 146).

frequently attracted support on quasi-charismatic grounds. This was true especially of the SA, where many local leaders were not merely commanders in a hierarchy acting under superior orders but leaders followed for their personal qualities. They received the allegiance of their subordinates not because of their rank in the hierarchy, but because they were respected (Bracher *et al.*, 1960, p. 844). Such instances could be found also among local party leaders, many of whom established their local Nazi groups without orders from Munich (Heiden, 1944, p. 301). They managed to develop a strong following for themselves and produced rigidly disciplined groups of fanatical fighters.[6]

The district leaders followed Hitler's example of disbursing offices on a personal basis. They developed networks of followers and protégés whom they constantly attempted to get into positions of power. This increased the intrigue and competition, since, in the absence of any strictly defined competences, their power was limited only by Hitler's trust in them (Rosenberg, 1955, pp. 166–168). The cleverness of the subleader and his ability to secure Hitler's confidence was the only determinant of his power (Gerth, 1940, p. 520).

The intriguing aspect of Hitler's organizational principle was that, although the subleaders had absolute authority within their delegated spheres, they did not necessarily have exclusive jurisdiction in their areas of operation. Hitler assigned overlapping jurisdictions without any institutional coordination and in the meantime emphasized absolute autonomy; the result was confusion and duplicated efforts. The principle of "double occupancy" in effect contradicted the principle of self-government and helped to make intraparty relations even more tenuous and competitive.[7] Characteristically, some of Hitler's subordinates also employed this device because they recognized its advantages. For example, Kersten has noted that Himmler gave new tasks not to the institutions already established for that purpose, but to individuals, and sometimes to several, who thereby became one another's rivals (Kersten, 1952, p. 261).

[6] See Hitler's remarks on Streicher's following in Nuremberg and Rosenberg's notes on Dinter's organization in Thuringia (Rosenberg, 1955, p. 96; Hitler, 1953, p. 126).

[7] Dietrich, 1955, p. 132. Occasionally, this situation evoked some bitter comments. Goebbels noted in his diary on January 5, 1932, that one of the major questions in any organization is the delimitation of competences. So long as this is not done, a cordial cooperation even among the best willed people is impossible. (Goebbels, 1937, p. 18.)

The exercise of self-government on the lower levels and the absolute authority of subleaders decentralized the movement territorially and functionally (Baumont *et al.,* 1955, p. 489). Leaders completely autonomous in their districts had no institutional ties to one another aside from the purely formal district leaders' conferences, discontinued after 1937 (Fest, 1963, p. 70). Before 1934, the SA and the party were wholly independent organizations, and other formations of the movement enjoyed similar independence and self-government.[8]

The sole central agent, the dynamic middle of the movement, was Hitler. In the absence of any coordinating mechanisms on the lower levels, he was the only meeting point for the little Hitlers, whose jealousies prevented any systematic, continuing cooperation on the secondary levels of leadership. The isolation of the subleaders was intensified by the fact that Hitler limited them strictly to their spheres of authority— they enjoyed autonomy, but at the same time they were absolutely restricted. This made Hitler the only one who had access to information about the movement as a whole. All lines converged on Hitler, who, in turn, was the only authoritative source of information for everybody else. Hitler was acutely conscious of the importance of such a position and took care to preserve it. "The wire reaches only as far as me," he is reported to have declared, implying that although he was informed about everything, he did not necessarily pass on to others what he knew (Olden, 1936, p. 186). "Bear in mind," he told Lüdecke, "that I have an old principle: only to say what must be said to him who must know it, and only when he must know it" (Lüdecke, 1938, p. 456).

These organizational devices contributed to the predominant position of the leader and also enhanced his charismatic authority. He was the only unifier for the disparate, competing elements of the movement. His omnipresence and omnipotence induced fear and admiration in his subordinates, eliciting such awestruck comments as Rosenberg's "Hitler seemed to know about everything. He had spiritual antennas and knew what one thought about things" (1955, pp. 159, 231).

Hitler's central position made him the only man who could settle disputes among the warring chieftains. He was the only one who had authority to coordinate the independent and quasi-autonomous organizations. Because all parties had to appeal to him, he could build up the

---

[8] Mau, 1953, p. 122. Suggestions concerning the subordination of SA units to local party organizations were repeatedly vetoed by Hitler (Reed, 1953, p. 80).

image of a man who had no special interests but only the interests of the whole. This separated him from all other leaders in the movement, who represented special views, organizations, or, frequently, nothing more than their own ambitions.

Hitler's separation from his subordinates was an essential part of his charismatic authority, for in the eyes of his followers he had to appear unique and fundamentally different from everybody else. This separation was furthered by Hitler's progressive withdrawal from administrative tasks, for which he had neither taste nor ability. His isolation increased the mystery of his person and contributed to his charisma. As early as October, 1925, Goebbels noted in his diary that Hitler was difficult to approach and was surrounded like a monarch (Heiber, n.d., p. 34). By 1929–1930 he "had become a great man difficult to access; he rarely spoke to, and even more rarely held discussions with subordinate leaders" (Olden, 1936, p. 209; Miltenberg, 1931, pp. 20–21). A few years later such important members of the Nazi elite as Rosenberg and Wilhelm Frick found it difficult to see him (Seraphim, 1956, p. 129; Kersten, 1952, p. 62).

Isolation may have been a fortuitous accident arising from the nature of the organization, but it also may have been Hitler's conscious policy. He may have wanted to "envelop himself in a veil of mystery and to cast an intriguing darkness around his person" in order to strengthen his charismatic appeal (Olden, 1936, pp. 186–187; Arendt, 1958, p. 373). This inaccessibility increased the competition among his lieutenants to belong to the immediate circle around him. When mere access to his person came to signify power and authority, Hitler may have achieved the ultimate in charismatic organization: association with him became the source of authority (cf. Trevor-Roper, 1947).

Max Weber suggested that a charismatic movement is characterized by an organization whose nature is personal and communal rather than impersonal and bureaucratic. Both the theory and the practice of National Socialism illustrated Weber's idea of a charismatic group. Hitler explicitly stated in *Mein Kampf* that he wanted an organization based on organic, not bureaucratic, lines, and in practice he "tried to substitute men for laws, personal judgement and responsibility for the rule-book and anonymity" (1939, pp. 846, 848; Koehl, 1960, p. 925). It is reasonable to suggest that if the Nazis had any historical example in the back of their minds, it was not the centralized, bureaucratic empire of the Romans, but the feudal organization of the Middle Ages. The idea of an elective king chosen for personal qualities appealed to them (Koehl, 1960, pp. 921–922; Neumann, 1965, p. 80; Rosenberg, 1932, p. 61; *id*, 1939, p. 118; Gerth, 1940, p. 520), whereas a system of abstract, impersonal rules and of hierarchy did not. The nature of the movement was aptly described by one of its principal lieutenants, Hans Frank, as an "above-institutional monocracy based on personality" (eine über-institutionelle Persönlichkeitsmonokratie) (Frank, 1953, p. 191).

Not an absolute monarch resting on institutional authority, Hitler held his power by manipulating a delicate system of checks and balances. Through a variety of means, he applied the principle of divide and conquer, which enabled him to emerge as the sole focus of loyalty in the movement (Gisevius, 1963, pp. 121–123, 138–139, 155ff; Görlitz & Quint, 1952, pp. 629–631; Miltenberg, 1931, p. 21; Koehl, 1960, p. 927).

IV

The Impact of Charisma on
Factional Conflicts

BEFORE commencing the analysis of the impact of charismatic authority on factional conflicts, I must define the term "faction," which has suffered a curious neglect in the literature of political science. Here, a "faction" will denote a group of people joined together to further some goal in opposition to some other group or groups within the same party (cf. Ranney & Kendall's definition of faction as "an element inside a party whose purpose is to control the personnel and policies *of the party*" (1956, p. 126)). The label "faction" will imply a certain permanence in the group, resting on some organizational basis that lends it a degree of independence and power. Finally, a faction will involve a basic issue or issues which supply the reason for its existence.

This definition of a faction permits us to distinguish factional conflicts from other kinds of intragroup disagreements that are personal and ephemeral and that revolve around issues of no more consequence than the status of a particular person or temporary clique. Richard Rose says, "Because they persist through time, factions can be distinguished from the ad hoc combinations of politicians in agreement upon one particular issue or at one moment in time" (1966, p. 319). Were "factionalism" defined so broadly as to include personal disputes of all kinds, the term would lose its analytical usefulness. In that case all political organizations would be teeming with "factions," since the absence of unanimity would automatically imply the existence of factions. Accordingly, factionalism in this study will denote those conflicts in the Nazi party that centered around issues affecting some basic party policy, that had some permanence, and that had some organizational independence and power. Conversely, this definition will not define as factional conflicts those personal intrigues, differences, and alliances that were omnipresent but generally did not have the attributes listed above.

Factions are related to legitimacy. Although it implies dissent on some important programmatic or ideological issues, a faction also suggests organized dissent within a basic framework of agreement. The existence of a faction is predicated on the continued existence of the original group of which the dissenting group is a faction. Factions are by definition parts of the larger group—that is, they partake of that "minimum of voluntary submission" which makes the group legitimate and enables it to survive. Thus, factions accept the source of authority and the prevailing type of legitimacy. Their purpose is not to challenge the type of legitimacy which holds the group together, but to offer alternatives to the prevailing policies. They are potentially, therefore, new interpreters of the existing source of authority rather than new sources.

In order to achieve power and influence in the group, factions have to attract support within it. The basic prerequisites of this end are the validity and practicability of their specific policy proposals and the success of their claim to be the true interpreters of the source of authority—be that an ideology, a charismatic leader, or anything else. Factions, in order to be successful, have to appear legitimate to the group as a whole—i.e., they have to appear to strive for the same ends on the basis of the same principles as the group as a whole. For this reason, factions have to avoid at all costs challenging the source of authority: the only way to their own legitimization is to appear as the true representative of that source.

The charismatic source of authority in the Nazi movement was, therefore, of decisive significance for the pattern of factional conflicts. Hitler was immune from factional attacks and was elevated above the factions that strove to legitimize themselves by claiming to be his true representatives. Instead of challenging Hitler's authority, the factions competed for his support. The charismatic source of authority placed factions on the secondary levels of leadership and elevated the charismatic leader to the position of broker, arbiter, and ultimate judge. Hitler was the polar star around whom all factions revolved and from whom they received legitimacy and power.

The rank-and-file support of the Nazi factions depended on the extent to which the factions could successfully claim Hitler's support and confidence. Once Hitler disowned a faction, he destroyed its legitimacy and whatever popular support it may have commanded in the party. The National Socialists followed Hitler, who, as the source of legitimacy, was the cohesive force, the only point of unity in the movement. If they followed factional leaders, they did so in the belief that these leaders represented Hitler's will and acted on his behalf. At the moment Hitler turned against a faction, to the amazement of outside observers, the apparently powerful factional leaders found themselves suddenly without power and authority. The popularity which they were supposed to have was destroyed as if it had never existed, and they disappeared, leaving the movement substantially intact and Hitler's authority unimpaired. For the members of the Nazi movement, Hitler was the sole legitimizing force; he incorporated the Weltanschauung of National Socialism.

Thus, contrary to conventional notions, the existence of factions per se did not imply a crisis in Nazi leadership. Hitler himself did not discourage factional activities for a number of reasons that will be examined below. On the contrary, he seemed occasionally to encourage them, partly because their constant appeal for his support enhanced his prestige in the movement. It was only under particular circumstances that he was obliged to intervene and put an end to a faction. But before I examine those situations, I shall analyze the Nazi Weltanschauung and the organizational setup as they affected the nature of factionalism.

THE WELTANSCHAUUNG AND FACTIONALISM

Although the vagueness and the lack of programmatic content of the Nazi Weltanschauung encouraged factions by permitting highly divergent interpretations of what National Socialism was or what it was meant to be, Hitler purposely condoned this confusion by leaving the Idea undefined. The Weltanschauung had to remain, in Hitler's words, "infinitely interpretable," and its ideational content problematical in order to serve the purposes of absolute, unrestricted charismatic authority. The charismatic leader could incorporate only an undefined idea which existed solely in his person. The Nazi Weltanschauung had to remain an "empty faith" (Arendt, 1958, p. 324) if the authority of

37

the leader was to be absolute. Once defined and given programmatic content, an idea becomes an ideology by which the leader's policies can be judged and evaluated—i.e., it becomes a source of authority displacing the charismatic legitimacy. This is what Hitler pointed out to Otto Strasser in 1930, when he told him that once he committed National Socialism to concrete ideological goals, his absolute leadership would be subject to continual questions and challenges (Strasser, *Ministersessel*, pp. 10, 17).

This characteristic of the Weltanschauung made National Socialism, at least until 1934, a "host of possibilities of the most varied kind" (Mohler, 1950, p. 66; Broszat, 1960, p. 7). From time to time the movement wavered in its direction from left to right, alternatively emphasizing its nationalist, socialist, conservative, or racial aspects. These fuzzy outlines encouraged people to see in National Socialism what they wanted to see. "One group within the N.S.D.A.P. saw in the swastika flag nothing but a new combination, a new form for the colors black, white, and red, while another group saw in this banner the red flag with the swastika."[1] At least until the assumption of power in 1933, wrote Hans Frank, "there were as many National Socialisms as there were leaders" (1953, pp. 184–185).

There was indeed a remarkably strong tendency of the members of the Nazi elite to identify National Socialism with their particular programmatic goals. Rosenberg regarded the *Myth of the Twentieth Century* as the fundamental element in the Nazi movement, whereas Rauschning identified Nazism with conservative principles until he realized his error and started calling the movement nihilistic. Feder regarded the abolition of interest as the focal point of National Socialism; the SA leaders Röhm and Pfeffer saw in Nazism a political instrument for the establishment of a military state. Dinter wanted to make the party the instrument of his *197 Theses*, whereas the Strasser brothers took the socialistic tenets of Nazism at their face value and regarded them as the basis of the movement.[2]

Hitler tolerated this diversity of views about the nature of the move-

[1] From the testimony of Hans Fritzsche at Nuremberg (*Trial*, Vol. XVII, p. 137).
[2] These people who wanted to attach some programmatic content to National Socialism were called by Hans Frank the "objectivists," as opposed to the "totalitarians" for whom National Socialism remained an "infinitely interpretable *Weltanschauung*," or an "empty faith" (1953, p. 99). Cf. Lüdecke, 1938, p. 213; Kersten, 1952, pp. 248–249; Thorwald, 1952, p. 12.

ment without committing himself to any of them. The most sharply conflicting ideas were allowed to coexist in the party, which enabled National Socialism to appeal to the most diverse groups and to collect into its ranks princes and blacksmiths, bureaucrats and intellectuals, legitimists and nihilists, racists, conservatives, communists, and social- ists. "The party," wrote Barbu, "like a river, moved right and left, to collect the waters from all over the place: from here a dynamic group of ex-officers, from there a mystic and romantic circle of intellectuals, an enthusiastic youth organization, or a group of frustrated business men . . ." (1956, p. 123). Programmatic diversity proved an excellent instrument for attracting those who wanted change and who were will- ing to ascribe to Nazism their particular ideals and aspirations.

Although Hitler permitted these divergent ideas to exist in the move- ment for purely opportunistic reasons during the "times of struggle," the proponents of these views firmly believed in the eventual victory of their particular programmatic goals. They refused to admit that the National Socialist Weltanschauung had no programmatic content, and most of them gave up the idea that their special conception of National Socialism would become the orthodox interpretation (Olden, 1936, p. 76). When by the end of the 1930's, but certainly by the early 1940's, it became evident that Hitler allowed ideas to exist in the movement only so long as they were not thought to be the ideological basis of the move- ment, National Socialism became for many of its early followers a movement "of disappointed aspirations" (Broszat, 1960, pp. 13–14). The Nazi Weltanschauung had to remain an empty faith; it had to deal only with issues no more specific than "questions of importance for centuries" in order to serve the totalitarian purposes of its charis- matic leader (Arendt, 1958, p. 324).

So long as the objectivists were content to present their ideas as a program but not as an ideology—that is, as a means but not as the end of National Socialism—they were allowed to propagate their ideas without interference from Hitler. Feder's and the Strasser brothers' socialistic appeals, Rosenberg's racial theories, Hans Frank's concep- tion of National Socialist legal codes, the SA leaders' militaristic ideals, all existed side by side during the 1920's and early 1930's. They all subscribed to the "National Socialist Idea," and they all claimed to be National Socialists, albeit each of them claimed to be its true repre- sentative. They all claimed to possess Hitler's support even when it was not offered and gathered their supporters on the basis of such claims. Thus, they were all "legitimate" under the all-encompassing umbrella of the Weltanschauung and its charismatic spokesman.

Of course, these objectivists completely misunderstood the nature of the charismatic Hitler movement which followed no one school of thought (Olden, 1936, pp. 208–209). Hitler refused to commit himself to any of them, yet he also refrained from disowning them as long as they did not threaten to become the source of authority in the party. Thus, he remained on top, removed from the competition of the lower levels and from programmatic disputes, and he remained the person identified with "National Socialism," who signified everything but was committed to nothing. In the eyes of the typical Nazi adherent, Hitler had the recipe for the realization of the Idea even though he never specified the content (Bracher *et al.*, 1960, pp. 841–842). He was sustained by a faith of his followers that was empty of concrete content, a faith that enabled total psychological identification with him precisely because it was not tied to specifics. This aspect of the totalitarian appeal was well recognized by Hitler, though it was missed by many of his program-minded lieutenants (Arendt, 1958, p. 324).

Under the circumstances, it was quite natural that when Hitler, the legitimizing force of National Socialism, decided to turn against a faction, his action meant its political death. At that moment the faction lost its legitimacy, and its leaders found themselves isolated in the movement and discredited among their followers. A faction had no chance of survival in opposition to Hitler—it could not claim to be National Socialist without his endorsement, tacit support, or toleration. For whatever importance the leaders of the faction may have attached to their program or interpretation of Nazism, their supporters identified National Socialism with Hitler, not with any particular program. This was one of the manifestations of charismatic legitimacy in the Nazi movement.

Thus, the nature of the Nazi Weltanschauung reduced factionalism to the level of programs, and the leader remained above these contests as the personification of the Nazi Idea. So long as factions did not attempt to forge an ideology out of their program by identifying their interpretation with the Weltanschauung, their activities did not challenge the charismatic source of authority and represented no threat to the unity of the movement.

THE EFFECTS OF NAZI ORGANIZATIONAL PRINCIPLES ON FACTIONALISM

The organizational setup of the movement significantly affected the pattern of factional conflicts. The continual and absolute dependence of every officeholder on Hitler's trust and confidence reinforced Hitler's position, and the perpetual conflicts and jealousies inherent in the organization divided the subleaders among themselves. The organizational devices of overlapping spheres of activity and limited jurisdictions perpetuated conflicts on the secondary levels and at the same time made Hitler the only arbiter. Keeping the leader's confidence and staying on top meant vicious competition among the subleaders. The absence of institutional ties introduced perpetual uncertainty and suspicion into their relations; the activities, plans, and motives of others were of constant concern among the lieutenants, since information about these matters had to be obtained deviously.

Although the conflicts were inherent in Hitler's organization, according to many observers, Hitler purposely distributed offices among rivals in order to foment quarrels among them. Hitler "does not like his subordinate leaders to be too friendly and confidential with each other," writes Olden, "he actually likes them to quarrel, for then his position as arbiter gains in importance" (1936, p. 185). Hitler has been accused of maneuvering his lieutenants into rival positions so that he would be unchallenged at the helm (Fest, 1963, p. 55; see also Heiden, 1944, p. 301; Jarman, 1956, p. 121; Rosenberg, 1955, p. 319; Drage, 1958, p. 73).

Hitler allowed his subleaders to be identified with certain political orientations, and he himself appeared to endorse all, but none exclusively. Thus, Göring, Röhm, and Pfeffer were identified with militaristic groups, the Strasser brothers with the workers, Göring and Dietrich with business circles and conservatives, Darré with the rural population, Rosenberg with racism. These may be seen as the tentacles of the movement attempting to reach practically all segments of the population. To the extent that these tentacles were incompatible, their representatives distrusted each other, not only because of conflicting convictions but also because their own fates seemed to be connected with the success of their points of view at the expense of the others. The ensuing rivalries were aggravated by the fact that the Nazi elite was composed of radically different personalities of varying class, religion, geography, and ideological dogma who were united only by the vague Idea of National Socialism, ambition, and political loyalty to Hitler.

The dissensions and bitter conflicts at the lower levels protected the leader from dangerous combinations against him. A subleader had his hands full with fighting his peers; he was concerned above all to discredit and defeat his immediate competitors and thereby raise his position. Hitler, meanwhile, could play one against the other and thereby remain on top. He was the only man capable of undoing the Gordian knot, the only man to whom all could appeal—to whom, indeed, all factions had to appeal (Dietrich, 1955, p. 132; Baumont *et al.*, 1955, p. 489).

Hitler's charisma, the Weltanschauung, and the organization of the party all perpetuated conflicts on the lower levels and elevated Hitler's tactic of neutrality—which, in turn, encouraged dissension among his lieutenants and supplied his image as the symbol of unity. The difficulty of obtaining his support increased its value as the prize of factional contention.

Hitler's refusal to commit himself until the last possible moment and his reluctance to make decisions were widely recognized by his subordinates, sometimes with exasperation. "Hitler hesitates to make a decision no matter how small," writes Otto Strasser (1948, p. 70); "In my conflict with Esser and Company, Hitler avoided any decision," writes Rosenberg (1955, p. 327). SA leader Stennes complained at the time of the SA crisis in 1930 that Hitler would not make any decision for weeks; "he always shirked making a decision" (Drage, 1958, p. 73). Goebbels's diary illustrates the exasperation of his co-workers with his indecisiveness. In connection with the question of Hitler's candidacy for the presidency in 1930, Goebbels made the following entries: January 19, "I am pleading for his candidacy." January 31, "The Führer's decision will be made Wednesday." February 2, "The Führer is deciding to run." February 9, "Everything is still in the air." February 12, "At last the decision has been made." February 18, "No decision yet." February 19, "The decision has been made." February 21, "The eternal waiting is almost demoralizing." February 22, "Hitler made his decision."[3]

It is an open question whether Hitler's reluctance to make decisions

[3] 1937, pp. 26–50. On his reluctance to take sides see Heiden, 1944, p. 369; Fest, 1963, p. 137; Hanfstängl, 1957, p. 118, Miltenberg, 1931, p. 21; Olden, 1936, p. 170; Strasser, 1938, p. 77.

was a personality trait or a deliberate tactic,[4] but this question is of little importance here. Whether it was intuitive, conscious, or inherent, Hitler's postponement of decisions and avoidance of commitments proved excellent tactics. The longer he held out, the more valuable his support and the more decisive his intervention. By staying out of the conflicts as long as possible, he preserved his image as the symbol of unity and increased his prestige. Without his intervention the conflicts among his subordinates usually ended in stalemates: success depended on Hitler's support. There was never any question that Hitler could, if he wanted to, resolve the conflicts; as the British Ambassador reported from Berlin, "there are rifts within the party, dissensions, jealousies . . . Nazis are heard to say: 'I am a Göring man' or a 'Goebbels man.' But Hitler has the power to restore unity if he wants to." (Woodward & Butler, Vol. V, No. 492 (October 25, 1933), p. 718; see also Frank, 1953, p. 47.)

Hitler's refusal to commit himself may have been irritating for his subordinates and could be interpreted as a personality trait by outside observers, but for the rank-and-file Nazi, it meant that Hitler stood above petty quarrels. This made him tower above his subordinate party leaders and furthered his isolation from them. It preserved his freedom of action and his independence. "Hitler listens to all, but is always free in his decisions," noted Rosenberg.[5]

THE NATURE OF FACTIONAL CRISES

Although Hitler's position as the source of authority as well as his organizational and tactical devices exempted him from direct entanglement in factional conflicts, there were exceptional cases where he became a party to conflicts and was forced to take a stand. In these instances, which may be labeled "factional crises," the conflicts shifted from the secondary levels and involved Hitler directly. It remains to

---

[4] Olden seems to subscribe to the former, Blank and Rosenberg to the latter.

[5] Seraphim, 1956, p. 131; Rosenberg, 1955, p. 319. Aside from decisions involving questions of ideology or policy, Hitler carefully avoided intervention in personality conflicts. He told Lüdecke that he did not concern himself with the private lives of his subordinates. He also disregarded corruption, which he considered secondary to discipline and loyalty. He did not care about corruption in the Berlin SA or in Röhm's circle and he was willing to forgive anything to old fighters like Streicher. "Despite all his weaknesses," he told his table companions, "he's [Streicher] a man who has spirit . . . He put himself under my orders at a time when others were hesitating to do so, and he completely conquered the city of our Rallies. That's an unforgettable service." (Lüdecke, 1938, p. 429; Hitler, 1953, p. 126.)

examine the circumstances under which such crises generally occurred and the manner of their resolution.

Hitler was drawn into factional disputes when one of his decisions was questioned and his absolute leadership challenged. For example, in 1926 the northern leaders passed a resolution opposing Hitler's policy on the expropriation of princes' property. Hitler, who had viewed the conflict between the northern party leaders and the Munich group throughout 1924–1925 from a position of neutrality, immediately intervened by convening the Bamberg conference. Similarly, the socialist orientation of the Kampfverlag circle was notorious from 1926 on, yet Hitler did not put a stop to their activities until the summer of 1930, when the Kampfverlag decided to dispute his decision about the strike in Saxony. Gregor Strasser's socialist views were well known to Hitler from 1920 on, but Strasser did not get into trouble until December, 1932, when he decided to follow a policy different from Hitler's on the issue of coalition government. Finally, the attitudes of the SA leadership around Röhm were hardly a matter of conjecture throughout the 1920's and early 1930's, yet Hitler moved against him and his circle only in June, 1934, when he believed that Röhm was plotting against him.

There is little doubt that in all these cases factional crises arose on issues of specific policy. Hitler tolerated divergent programmatic positions so long as his authority was not challenged. As was argued above, his authority was not jeopardized by these different conceptions of National Socialist programs; hence, there was no reason to make an issue of them. This was amply illustrated at the time of the factional crises, when Hitler seemed to care only about the specific issue of policy, not about the broader issues propagated by the particular factions. Thus, at the Bamberg conference the socialist issue remained unresolved, but there was no doubt about the stand of the party on the expropriation question. In the summer of 1930, Hitler was not interested in a discussion of the broad ideological differences between Otto Strasser and himself, but in the specific policy of the Kampfverlag toward the strike in Saxony. In 1932, he never mentioned Gregor Strasser's socialistic views: his invectives were exclusively directed to Strasser's treasonable negotiations with General Schleicher. In 1934 the broader implications of the "second revolution" were never discussed; the issue was Röhm's alleged conspiracies against Hitler. In each case, the issues were reduced to tactical questions of specific policy, which permitted compromise and preserved party unity in the crisis. Also, Hitler could act conciliatorily —as an arbiter rather than as a victor. The programmatic heterogeneity in the movement continued, which was important for electoral purposes. And Hitler could escape ideological discussions that would have implied by definition that his position as the source of authority was in question.

The characteristic feature of the crises of 1926 and of 1930 was that Hitler appeared as an arbiter intent on conciliation and compromise, not as a victor intent upon punishment. The factional leaders of the north were not punished in 1926, nor were the leaders of the Kampfverlag in 1930. Otto Strasser quit the party in 1930 against Hitler's wishes. When his brother Gregor resigned from his offices in 1932, remaining in the party, not one of his close associates was purged by Hitler. The "purge" of 1934 was not a purge of the SA in any systematic sense, although in this case Hitler appeared least conciliatory for a number of reasons that will be analyzed below.

Hitler's conciliatory policy at the time of the crises cannot be interpreted as merely expeditious in order to avoid party splits at those crucial moments. The factional leaders of 1926, 1930, or 1934 did not suffer any punishment after Hitler was securely in power. Past participation in factional conflicts did not seem to affect the careers of Nazi functionaries, some of whom rose to high positions. Among these were Koch, Kaufmann, Rust, Goebbels, and Lutze, who were prominent in the northern movement of 1925; Brückner and Helldorff, who were Röhm's confidants in 1924–1925; Hinkel and Buchrucker, who belonged to the inner circle of the Kampfverlag; Frick and Ley, who supported Gregor Strasser in 1932; and Himmler, who was for a time Gregor Strasser's secretary.

The reduction of broader issues to questions of tactics also helped to deprive factional leaders of any support they might otherwise have obtained. Undoubtedly, this was not the major reason for the loyalty of the rank and file to Hitler at the time of the crises, but it may have been a contributory cause. Disagreement on tactics could hardly excite the enthusiasm of the ordinary party member, who was notoriously unconcerned about means. Thus, there was little reason to follow the factional leader rather than Hitler in crises. After all, Hitler did not attack the program of the faction, merely one of its policies. Respected factional leaders were not excommunicated, were not vilified. Hence, the movement could survive factional crises without splits or mass purges, and Hitler could shine as the healer of factional conflicts and the guardian of party unity; factional crises were settled on the highest levels of leadership, involved a handful of people, and left the mass of members and followers unaffected.

The tactical nature of the issues permitted a conciliatory policy, but it also perpetuated programmatic heterogeneity. In this sense the factional crises were inconclusive as far as the resolution of the real issues was concerned. Thus, the socialist issue did not cease to be an aspect of Nazism either after the crisis of 1926 or that of 1930, nor was the controversy over the military resolved in 1934. Hitler was not interested in resolving these issues finally so long as they proved useful recruiting tools in the struggle for power. Hitler did not care about dogmatic consistency; he appealed to the masses who wanted psychological identification with a cause and a utopian idea more than they wanted ideological consistency.

The pattern of factional conflicts may be summarized under the following points:

(1) Charismatic authority elevated the leader above factional conflicts among the secondary leadership.

(2) Factions claimed to be Hitler's representatives in order to legitimize themselves in the movement. Thus, they were not directed against Hitler, but competed for his support.

(3) Factions could count on rank-and-file support only as long as they could represent themselves as acting on Hitler's behalf. Once they came into conflict with Hitler, their supporters deserted them, and the faction collapsed.

(4) Factions attached themselves to programmatic issues, whereas Hitler was identified with the remote Weltanschauung. So long as Hitler did not specifically disown a programmatic position, factions could continue to propagate their views without impairing his authority. The heterogeneity of programs helped Nazism to gather support from all quarters although the aims of the movement remained undefined by Hitler.

(5) The organization of the movement reinforced the conflicts on the secondary levels and elevated Hitler above them. It also divided the Nazi elite by making everyone dependent on Hitler.

(6) Hitler's tactic of neutrality perpetuated conflicts and increased his authority as ultimate arbiter and benevolent judge.

(7) Factional crises occurred on questions of specific policy, not on issues of program. The leader moved against a faction when his orders were contested, but he acted as a benevolent arbiter, not as a victor. This conciliatory behavior kept factional leaders in the movement and prevented party splits.

(8) The mass of members remained unaffected by factional conflicts, which were settled at the level of leadership. This also prevented splits and made mass purges unnecessary.

I shall subject these generalizations to the test of historical evidence in Part Two. The discussion will be organized around the two major factional groupings of the northerners (consisting of the crises of 1926 and 1930) and around the SA faction. Although the years 1919–1925 are outside the scope of this study for reasons that will be explained, a brief discussion of the period before 1925 is desirable not only because it will give historical background and continuity, but also because those years contain the germs of future factional conflicts.

卐 PART TWO

THE HISTORY OF FACTIONAL CONFLICTS

V

Prelude to the
Mass Movement, 1919–1925

A HISTORICAL account of the factional conflicts is necessary even in this essentially analytic study because no definitive history of Nazi factionalism has yet been written. As a consequence, the issues, the sequence of events, and the participants' attitudes and motivations are all open to dispute as will be apparent in the course of the following discussion. Historical data are open to several interpretations, and some of those arrived at in this study are radical departures from more generally accepted ones.

This analysis of the history of factional conflicts has been restricted to 1925–1934. Such a delimitation is by no means entirely arbitrary, for 1925 and 1934 represent significant turning points in the history of the Nazi movement. Before 1925, National Socialism was in its formative stages, and this period was in many respects its pre-totalitarian phase. The organization of an independent, tightly disciplined party based on the leadership principle became a matter of conscious policy only after 1925. It was during his imprisonment that Hitler defined his thoughts about the nature and organization of the party; before that he was more a soldier of fortune trying to exploit existing situations and planning *coups d'état* than a professional revolutionary creating conditions favorable for his purposes. After 1925 the Nazi movement assumed its independence and ceased to be an appanage of *völkisch* and military circles; at that time the movement began to acquire a mass base of followers and a well-defined organizational structure. The Nazis implemented the idea of a totalitarian party only after 1925, the date which marks the beginning of the charismatic mass movement.

The year 1934 was similarly significant in the history of the movement, for it represented the conclusion of the *Kampfzeit,* the period of the struggle for power. Until 1934 National Socialism had, in the eyes of its followers and non-followers alike, unlimited possibilities. The nature of its Weltanschauung allowed the coexistence of the most diverse groups within the movement, each secretly (and sometimes openly) believing that the movement, now representing many differing ideas and political orientations, would ultimately embrace its particular point of view. The testimony of Hans Fritzsche before the Nuremberg tribunal is particularly revealing in this connection:

When I joined the NSDAP, I believed I was joining such a movement because one group within the NSDAP saw in the swastika flag nothing but a new combination, a new form for the colors black, white, and red, while another group saw in this banner the red flag with the swastika. It is a fact that there were whole groups of the former German Nationalist Party in the NSDAP or of former Communists in the NSDAP. [*Trial,* Vol. XVII, p. 137.]

The year 1934 put an end to such hopes and illusions: in that year rose the "Order State," which was more concerned with the solution of existing problems ("the principle of the execution of orders at any price") than with the utopian future. In the years after 1934 it became clear to all willing to see and listen that the Nazi state was not to be a socialistic state, nor a military state, nor a state based on traditional ideas of authority, but a state based on the concept of order.[1] Order became sacred regardless of its substance, and loyalty became equated with obedience.

The following historical analysis concerns the pre-power years of the

---

[1] I am using "order" in the Nazi sense to denote the end of the revolutionary period of the struggle for power (Kampfzeit) and the beginning of the new order. The Nazis glorified order after their assumption of power and frequently referred to their state as the "Order State." The SS was officially proclaimed an "order" in 1936 (Neusüss-Hunkel, 1956, p. 19) and "Ordensburgen" were established as educational institutions for the future Nazi elite (Kogon, 1960, pp. 13–14). Their emphasis on obedience reflected the Nazis' concept of order as well as their static conception of the future. See also pp. 140–141 below.

But order is glorified by all types of post-revolutionary totalitarians as well as by the Nazis. Arthur Koestler quotes the statement of a young Soviet official: "We are not believers. Not as you are. We do not believe either in God or in men. We manufacture gods and we transform men. We believe in Order." (1954, pp. 155–156).

totalitarian Nazi movement. It was during this period that factions arose and the significant factional crises took place. The factional crises of 1926, 1930, and 1934 were landmarks in the history of the movement that affected the nature and orientation of National Socialism in the years to come. Neither before 1925 nor after 1934 were there factional conflicts of corresponding significance. The great issues about the nature and political orientation of the party that motivated factional conflicts came into the open only between 1925 and 1934. Before this period the party (if one can call it that) was too much part of the amorphous völkisch movement, it was too involved in the idea of a putsch, it had to fight too hard to preserve its identity to be concerned with issues of leadership, organization, and political orientation. After 1934 power had been captured, and the party turned from questions of principle to questions of practical politics. Thus, the era of factional conflicts was basically the period 1925–1934.

卐　　卐　　卐

The dissatisfied masses of postwar Germany could choose between two major forces in order to escape their dire predicament: the völkisch nationalist Weltanschauung of the right and the Marxist international ideology of the left. Each of these offered simple solutions to complex problems; each promised its particular utopia to those who were in need of one. Unfortunately for the Weimar system, the number of those who wanted simple answers and radical changes continued to increase in the postwar period, with only temporary reverses in the mid-1920's. The system and its institutions failed to attract the loyalty of the masses, thus making them eager recipients of these two potentially totalitarian appeals. By the early 1930's the national forces of the right and the Marxist forces of the left dominated German politics. The Weimar system, divorced from the national tradition, did not impart a sense of purpose and had little chance of survival between these two powerful grindstones. Without an ideological base or inspired leadership, the Weimar Republic could not be a third force; it was too encumbered by procedural deadlocks and adverse international pressures to compete with its totalitarian enemies. By the end of the 1920's, men began to question whether the forces of the right or the left would inherit the German states. This simple dichotomy was opportune for the Nazis, who, unlike their Marxist opponents, could exploit national traditions and at the same time offer something entirely new and untried under the leadership of a demagogic genius who could capture the imagination of the masses. The Nazis won the state for two additional reasons: their leadership was flexible and opportunistic enough to adjust to the situations of the moment, and they had allies and sympathizers among those in important positions of power who would ultimately tip the balance in their favor.

Of the several reasons for the success of the National Socialists none seems to have been more important than their successful claim to the leadership of the "national" forces of Germany. The tool that made this identification was the völkisch idea, which the Nazis managed to turn to their own purposes. The importance of this idea for the National Socialist movement has received minimal recognition among non-German writers; indeed, many non-German accounts of National Socialism fail to mention it. In contrast, the role of the völkisch idea has received considerable emphasis in German writings about National Socialism.[2]

Although frequently translated as "racism,"[3] the term "völkisch" comes closer to tribal populism or integral nationalism with tribal overtones. After 1918, the völkisch concept became a slogan of numerous political forces in Germany and provided a broad umbrella for the diverse right-wing groups fighting against the established political system. There was hardly another concept that carried so many associations, possibilities, and meanings (Broszat, 1958, pp. 56, 84). The idea was adopted by the members of the old ruling circles, the conservatives, and the professional military who all wanted the restoration of the *status quo ante bellum*, as well as by the ex-soldiers, Free Corps men, and the youth who all wanted a new order roughly in the form of the war community of comrades, a community of equals united as one man and devoted to an all-encompassing purpose. The former group used the völkisch idea to justify the restoration of autocracy and the preservation of vested in-

---

[2] See the writings of, among others, Hannah Arendt, Martin Broszat, Godfried Neesse, Kurt Lüdecke, Weigand von Miltenberg (Herbert Blank), Rudolf Olden, Karl O. Paetel. The speeches and memoirs of Nazi leaders provide additional illustrations of the importance that they attached to the idea.

[3] Such a translation would be applicable to the concept as used by anti-Semitic groups in the nineteenth century. They narrowed the idea to suit their purposes and identified it with racial nationalism to make their argument that the Jews could not be integrated into the nation conclusive. (Reichmann, 1951, pp. 53–54.)

terests; the latter group saw in the idea the promise of a classless community of equals set apart from others by an aggressive and exclusive nationalism. In the völkisch concept one can find practically all the ideas of National Socialism: anti-Semitism, community, blood and soil, and the myth of a New Germany.

The völkisch idea was an ideal demagogic tool for the Nazis, who utilized it extensively to describe the cultural, literary, philosophic, and religious as well as the political elements of their Weltanschauung (Broszat, 1958, p. 57). The obscure and infinitely malleable idea fit the Nazi concept of Weltanschauung; it did not limit the principle of absolute leadership as an ideology would have done, and its esoteric nature required interpretation for the masses, thus allowing for charismatic legitimacy.

The popular, albeit undefined idea suited Nazi political aims because it could serve as a common symbol for the diverse national-minded groups with occasionally conflicting aims. It could appeal to all who wanted change in the nationalistic direction by obscuring the specifics of national integration. Its utopian message enabled the Nazis to stay on the offensive, and its lack of concrete content made it an elusive target of criticism. By exploiting the völkisch idea, the Nazis could play a double role: to the politically underprivileged they promised new political influence and to the traditional ruling classes they offered a new popular base. As a result, the idea let the movement appear as an organic synthesis of the masses and the elite.

The intellectual history of the völkisch idea goes back to the nineteenth century, when it was discovered by some radical conservatives who were worried about the problem of integrating the newly enfranchised masses into the national community. Up to the First World War the idea failed to gain substantial political support, but it was associated with several advanced intellectual circles, which lent it considerable prestige and respectability. The experience of the war and the problems of postwar Germany gave the idea tremendous impetus and transformed it into a political force. Unlike many nineteenth-century ideas that became meaningless and outdated for large numbers of people in the confused period 1914–1923, the völkisch idea was strengthened by the experiences of these years. In the postwar period, numerous groups, among them the Nazis, claimed the idea as their intellectual basis and assumed the common but vague identity of "national-minded" groups[4] under the völkisch banner.

In this early period of National Socialism, the party was explicitly distinguished from the völkisch movement, although Hitler never ceased struggling to have his party recognized as the principal carrier of the movement. It is important to stress that up to the time of his imprisonment Hitler and his followers saw themselves only as the principal exponents of the broader völkisch movement and did not think of exclusive power for their party. It was only during his imprisonment that Hitler realized that he must not allow himself to become dependent on any broader organization; it was then that he conceived of a totalitarian party based on the principles of exclusive and total power and of absolute leadership. At the same time, he concluded that his party must be either identified with the völkisch movement or separated from it. By the 1930's he had successfully identified the party with the movement (Franz, 1957, p. 319). At that point, after its temporary demise in the mid-1920's, the völkisch idea became prominent again in Nazi pronouncements.

The attitude of the Nazis toward the völkisch idea before 1924 illustrates that of a radical group seeking change within the traditional frame of reference, and their attitude after 1924 that of a totalitarian group operating by exclusiveness. Before 1924 Nazi totalitarian principles were hardly formulated, and only a few of them were practiced in a rudimentary, unsystematic manner. The eschatological character of its Weltanschauung was encumbered with the twenty-five-point program; its leadership principle was not complemented by any strong charismatic qualities; its members were mostly persons who saw in the party not a new beginning, but a continuation of old ideologies or interests. For these reasons, the party before 1924 cannot really be called totalitarian, and it is therefore of only marginal significance for a study of the patterns of factional conflicts in a totalitarian movement based on charismatic legitimacy.

However, one may discern certain parallels between the issues raised by the factions after 1925 and the conflicts in the party from 1919 to

[4] In the postwar years such intellectual circles as the *Thule* Society and the *Tatkreis* adopted the völkisch idea as their fundamental concept (Franz, 1957, pp. 326–328). On the intellectual history of the concept in the nineteenth century, see Stern, 1961.

1924, and for this reason this period is of interest for this book. Although the conflicting party groupings of this period do not satisfy the definition of factions in Chapter IV, they do provide a historical background for the factional conflicts of the later period.

Three major intraparty conflicts may be seen in this early period of party history. The first was between the founders of the German Workers' party and the new party leadership headed by Hitler and Ernst Röhm. This conflict came to a climax in the summer of 1921, and Hitler's group won. The second conflict, which did not come to a corresponding climax and resolution during this early period, was between the military arm of the party and the political leadership. The third conflict arose in connection with the May, 1924, elections, over the issue of political tactics.

These conflicts brought to the foreground, respectively, issues of the nature and political orientation of the party, of Ernst Röhm and the role of the Stormtroops, and of Gregor Strasser and the North German wing of the NSDAP. The issue about the nature and political orientation of the movement came to another climax in 1930, culminating in the dissolution of the Kampfverlag and the secession of the Otto Strasser group. The issue of the Stormtroops plagued the party leadership until its resolution in the purges of June, 1934. The issue of political tactics and the northern wing of the movement was raised at the Hanover congress in 1926 and again in December, 1932. In 1926 the northerners were defeated by Hitler; in 1932 Gregor Strasser resigned from his high party offices.

I imply no direct genealogy by drawing these parallels. The political context of the years 1919–1924 was too radically different from that of the later period to permit issues and lines of division to continue in the same form and substance. Yet the issues in their broadest sense were the same in both periods and touched upon some of the most important aspects of the movement.

THE NATURE AND POLITICAL ORIENTATION OF THE NSDAP

The striking feature of the German Workers' party (DAP), founded by Anton Drexler in January, 1919, was its humble definition of its role. It had no independent aspirations for power and conceived itself as merely a political vehicle for national unity. The party leaders declared in the "Directions of January 1919" that all they wanted was "to be ruled by Germans."[5] This recognition of the traditional political elite revealed the class-bound character of the DAP as well as its nineteenth-century, nationalistic political orientations.

The purpose of the party was to contribute to the creation of a united Germany based on the principles of freedom, equality, and fraternity. The divisive class war was to yield to integrating nationalism; the gap between the classes would be bridged by mutual understanding and respect. The DAP justified itself as a particularly useful tool for the realization of this national purpose. It was a party of employees, workers, and the "politically homeless" (Bölke, 1930, p. 361) who desired national integration instead of class divisions. It was a party with a concern for the interests of both the bourgeoisie and the socialists, thus presumably an ideal agency to enlighten both classes about their common destiny. The task of the party was conceived to be twofold: to bring back the workers to the national fold by liberating them from Marxist internationalism, and to make the upper classes aware of their social responsibilities. The workers had to be shown that "nationalism was the highest duty also for Socialists" (Drexler, 1937, p. 7), and the upper classes had to be made to realize that the way to national integration lay partly in recognition of the workers' social and political rights.

Although the DAP declared itself to be a socialist party dedicated to the "ennobling of the worker," its socialistic demands were justified as means to "higher," nationalistic ends. Similarly, freedom, equality, and fraternity were not to be ends in themselves, but were justified as the proper means to national integration.

At its inception, the DAP was composed of people of working-class origins who saw themselves in a humble role. There is no suggestion in the writings of Drexler that he ever thought of political power for himself or for his organization. He did not think of a party; the requisites of political organization—such as discipline, regular payment of dues, continuous propaganda, and active recruitment—were completely foreign to him.[6] His group was an educational organization in the service

[5] "Richtlinien der Deutschen Arbeiterpartei vom 5 January 1919," in Michaelis & Schraepler, n.d., pp. 212–214.
[6] On February 25, 1921, Drexler described his political attitude in the motto: "Nothing for myself, nothing for the Party, everything for my poor discredited people." Drexler's handwritten note is in the files of the University of California, Los Angeles, Department of Special Collections.
Harrer, then the first chairman of the DAP, opposed Hitler's idea to transform the

of a higher purpose—that is, at least until the middle of 1919, when it was transformed into a political organization by Hitler and Röhm.

The humble, idealistic foundation of the German Workers' party attracted certain right-wing circles that realized the importance of a popular base for political action. The first such group was the military. Soon after the recapture of Munich from the Communists in May, 1919, Röhm and several of his army comrades joined the DAP, and within a short time transformed the workers' discussion circle into a party of soldiers (Röhm, 1928, p. 107; Heiden, 1935, pp. 30–31; Waite, 1952, p. 93). As a result of the influx of soldiers and ex-soldiers, the organization rapidly lost its working-class character, and discussion gave way to emphasis on action. The new members from the military were full of their experiences in the war years, intense nationalism, and activism. They also brought with them "front socialism," the ideal of which was an anti-class, egalitarian community (Rosenberg, 1955, p. 90; Waite, 1952, p. 26). These new members infused military values of discipline, leadership, and organization, manifested by such outward symbols as the Fascist salute, uniforms, and the swastika. These ex-soldiers represented the new masses (Schäfer, 1957, p. 6). Their loss of former attachments coupled with the soldierly virtues of obedience and willingness to engage in physical violence made them ideal material in the hands of a new leader. They wanted a new order, but they were content to leave the particulars to their leader.[7]

Concurrently with the influx of soldiers into the party, and perhaps partly as a result of it, a number of intellectuals, ideologists, and professional men joined also. Hitler himself joined in September, after he had been sent out by his military commander to investigate Drexler's

DAP into a political party. In January, 1920, when Hitler's idea triumphed, Harrer left the DAP. (Franz-Willing, 1962, p. 68.)

The character of the DAP as a mere discussion circle is described by Czech-Jochberg: "They met once a week in a small café, but there were always the same people. They did not need convincing; they were convinced already. They did not go out to win the masses." (1933, p. 69.)

[7] On the mentality of ex-soldiers see Posse, 1931, p. 5 and *passim;* Waite, 1952, pp. 26, 115; Heiden, 1935, pp. 41–43, and the writings of Ernst Jünger, who characterized them as "die verlorene Haufe" or the lost mass or multitude (quoted in Waite, 1952, p. 115). Paul Szende, analyzing the psychology of veterans, pointed out that young people who during the war were arbiters over life and death were unwilling to be integrated into the work routine after the war. They dreamed of being a privileged elite and gave themselves wholeheartedly to the revolutionary romanticism of the Nazis and similar groups. (Szende, 1920–1921, pp. 337–375.)

party.[8] Gradually the leadership of the party was taken over by military men and another group, the "armed bohemians"—ideologists, adventurers, dissenters of all kinds, failures, and underworld characters (Arendt, 1958, p. 317; Schumann, 1958, pp. 30–31). The new coterie of "excitable, reckless even dubious characters" started to gather about Hitler and, under his and Röhm's leadership, transformed the party into an organization far different from that imagined by its founders (Heiden, 1935, p. 45; Bullock, 1959, p. 66).

Both in its effective leadership and in its composition the party ceased to be an organization of the lower classes, although it continued to make its appeal to them.[9] The leaders of the party assumed an elite consciousness that became increasingly apparent in their political activities. The organization of defense sections, extensive propaganda, active recruitment, and the acquisition of a party paper illustrate the changed political conceptions motivating the new party leadership.[10] These measures were principally Hitler's and Röhm's. Wholly conscious of his contribution to the rise of the party, certain of the military, and contemptuous of the old party leadership, Hitler began to assume full control over party policies and, by his own admission, to disregard the elected leader. He stayed away from committee meetings and refused to submit his decisions to discussion or to majority vote, thereby violating the constitutional provisions of the party (Hitler, 1939, pp. 857–858). Toward the end of 1920 his personal glorification began, first privately among his closest collaborators and then at public meetings. This glorification affected Hitler, who soon "began to believe in himself" (Heiden, 1935, pp. 39, 45).

By 1921 it became increasingly clear to the elected, *de jure* leaders

[8] On September 12, 1919, Hitler attended a public meeting of the DAP at which Gottfried Feder talked on the topic "How and with what means can one destroy capitalism?" His speech was followed by a separatist appeal of a Professor Baumann, which Hitler answered from the floor in a fifteen-minute rebuttal. Drexler was impressed by his delivery and arguments and whispered to the party secretary: "My friend, this one has what it takes, we could use him [Mensch, der hat a Gosch'n, den kunnt ma braucha]." A few days later Hitler joined the party. (Franz-Willing, 1962, pp. 66–67.)

[9] Red was the predominant color in Nazi posters and on Nazi flags (Hitler, 1939, pp. 506–507). In his table conversations Hitler talked about this problem: "I saw to it that all the initiates of the movement came to meetings without stiff collars and without ties, adopting the free and easy style so as to get the workers into their confidence" (Hitler, 1953 (April 8, 1942), p. 335).

[10] During 1920, eighty mass meetings were held and membership increased to around three thousand (Görlitz & Quint, 1952, p. 151).

of the party that Hitler's policies not only corrupted the original purposes of the DAP but also took away their power. The issue was brought into the open in July, 1921, when the old leaders rebelled against the domination of the Hitler clique. Their abortive attempt to recapture the party leadership led to reorganization of the party and the lawful recognition of Hitler as leader. The opportunity to bring into the open his latent conflict within the higher echelons came when Hitler was in Berlin expanding his ties with the North German nationalist groups. The revolt involved two basic issues: (1) concern over Hitler's increasing identification of the party with the right and his transformation of the party into a military organization, and (2) concern over Hitler's dictatorial methods and leadership. Hearing of the revolt, Hitler immediately returned from Berlin and demanded that his absolute leadership over party policies be recognized. Otherwise, he threatened, he would resign. The old leaders countered by an appeal to the rank and file in a leaflet attacking Hitler and some of his immediate associates. It deplored Hitler's "lust for power" and his attempt to use the party "as a springboard for his own immoral purposes, and to seize the leadership in order to force the Party on to a different track" (Heiden, 1935, p. 51). At the two extraordinary party meetings called to settle the conflict, Hitler won a complete victory. Drexler was obliged to repudiate the leaflet, and the convention granted Hitler the authority to reorganize the party and to substitute the principle of personal responsibility for that of decisions by vote of the majority.

Hitler won because his extraordinary contributions to the development of the party had gained him the support of the members, some of whom began to see in him the personification of the party and its ideals (Olden, 1936, pp. 107–108). He had behind him the army, with its funds and members, as well as the intellectuals and the party paper. His opponents, the original founders of the DAP, were people of limited ability and imagination, without mass appeal and influential allies (Heiden, 1935, p. 53; Görlitz & Quint, 1952, p. 146).

The victory of July 29, 1921, introduced into the party the principle of absolute leadership. This meant vesting complete authority in the leader (First Chairman). Decisions were no longer to be made in committee meetings, but by the leader alone or by his appointees to whom he might delegate specific powers. All authority was derived from the leader, to be used and delegated at his discretion.[11]

The fate of the old leadership was sealed in July, 1921. The representatives of the original DAP passed from the scene, and the "armed bohemians" took over. These were ambitious, dedicated men who refused to see themselves in a humble role. They had no respect for any traditional elite, but considered themselves the elite that ought to rule. According to them, a new order could not be built on old foundations; they did not think that much could be achieved by re-educating the old classes. They favored activism and force and started talking about the "new man" of the new order.[12] They were also attracted by the idea of personal leadership—i.e., by the rule of persons, not of institutions or principles. Thus, they prepared the ground for charismatic leadership. The traditions of the DAP were rapidly abandoned.[13]

Yet, despite their radicalism, the new leaders of the years 1921–1923 were to a certain extent still prisoners of the old political framework. For one thing, they continued to use rightist political tactics and thought of revolution as coming about from above by intrigue instead of from below by the organization of the masses.[14] Hitler and his associates were preoccupied with the idea of the putsch and neglected the mass organization of the party. They still thought of exploiting the political situation, instead of creating situations favorable to their ends.[15] The image they held of themselves as part of a broader movement made them unconcerned about ideas. "It is no business of mine," Hitler is reported to have

[11] Hitler, 1939, p. 858, and the testimony of Major Frank B. Walter at Nuremberg, *Trial*, Vol. II, pp. 180–183.

[12] "We are not going to be saved by going back to the old, to the Reaction, to the generals and excellencies, but by the men of action, the youth and the front soldiers" (Röhm, 1928, p. 255).

[13] The DAP concept of leadership was contained in Feder's letter to Hitler of August 10, 1923. Criticizing Hitler's autocratic behavior, he wrote: "We gladly yield first place to you as long as it is a first place among equal and free men in accordance with the best Germanic traditions. But we miss in you the recognition of the necessity of a closer contact with your colleagues and the people who are working for the same cause . . . We all want to be servants of the State, in the spirit of Frederick the Great; we gladly yield first place to you; but for tyrannical tendencies we have no understanding." (Hale, 1958, p. 362).

[14] "I can confess quite calmly," said Hitler in 1936, "that from 1919 to 1923 I thought of nothing other than a *coup d'état*" (speech of November 9, 1936, in Baynes, 1942, Vol. I, p. 154. On the "putschist mentality" see Mannheim, 1936, pp. 141ff.

[15] Until the putsch of 1923, writes Lüdecke, Hitler had been riding a wave of national despair with the support of the army (1938, p. 304).

said in 1923, "to found a new philosophy. My problems are purely practical and political." (Hanfstängl, 1957, p. 84.) The party of 1923 fell far short of a totalitarian organization. These shortcomings were recognized publicly by Hitler some years later:

But fate meant well with us; fate did not allow an action to succeed, which, if it had succeeded must in the end have suffered shipwreck on the internal unpreparedness of the movement, on its organization which was then so faulty, on its inadequate spiritual foundations . . . Then we played our part only with courage and bravery. . . .[16]

After his release from prison, Hitler set out to correct these shortcomings. The failure of the putsch was not lost on him. He recognized that it made little sense to overthrow the state without having a new state ready at hand to replace it.[17] The party had to be organized so that it would parallel the institutions of the state.

THE ROLE OF THE STORM DIVISIONS IN THE NSDAP

The idea behind the organization of the strong-arm division in 1920[18] rested on the recognition that propaganda coupled with terror is more effective than propaganda without terror. Hitler recognized early the attractiveness of power and force for the masses and their utility for a political organization. His views about the armed sections of the party were always political; the divisions were to be an instrument of power for political ends.

At the same time, the increasing dependence of the party on the forces of the right in general and the military in particular affected the development of the armed divisions.[19] Soon they were to acquire military characteristics, not only in such outward symbols as uniforms but also in organizational form. By late 1921 the SA was beginning to come under the influence of professional military men. Its membership, formerly ruffians of all kinds, began to rise rapidly because of enlistment

[16] From Hitler's speech of November 8, 1935, in Baynes, 1942, Vol. I, p. 133.

[17] See Hitler's speech of November 9, 1936, in Baynes, 1942, Vol. I, p. 155.

[18] There were several changes in the designations of these strong-arm divisions. Initially they were called "Defense Sections." Then, in August, 1921, they were renamed the "Gymnastics and Sports Sections." After October, 1921, they were known as the "Storm Sections." (Baynes, 1942, Vol. I, p. 171.)

[19] The first recruiting proclamation of the SA declared that the organization "will embody and propagate the military idea of a free nation." The proclamation is quoted in part in Heiden, 1935, p. 107.

of entire Free Corps units under former officers (Röhm, 1928, p. 109; Lüdecke, 1938, pp. 78ff; Bracher *et al.*, 1960, pp. 832ff).

The increasingly critical nature of foreign and domestic politics in Germany after 1922 made the SA more important. The SA became the center of the party; more and more often it represented the party at festive occasions by marching through towns in demonstrations (Schäfer, 1957, p. 7). But as the SA came to assume an important role in the party, its military tendencies endangered Hitler's position. The conflict between Hitler's conception of absolute leadership and Röhm's military conception of the SA became obvious. For Hitler, especially after July, 1921, the SA was a party organization serving party ends and was responsible to him. Whereas Hitler thought of a new political order, whose establishment had to precede the build-up of a national army, Röhm thought of a military state, where the soldier would come first and politics would at best be a necessary, if temporary, evil. Hitler and Röhm agreed in their common opposition to the Republic, to Marxism, and to the "Reaction," but their views of the new order differed significantly until June 30, 1934, when Röhm was shot on Hitler's orders and the SA was demoted in the Nazi hierarchy.

With his military bias, Röhm never accepted Hitler's argument that the organization of a national army would have to wait until the new order had been established. Being a military man, Röhm thought the organization of a national army was the prerequisite of a new order. He wanted to collect all military groups—including the SA—into a national organization as the basis of the future state. He refused to recognize Hitler's claim that the SA was first of all a party organ, subservient to the party leadership.

Röhm's first chance to act on his ideas came with the Ruhr occupation. During January and February, 1923, the SA was reorganized into a paramilitary formation with its own supreme commander (Bracher *et al.*, 1960, p. 836). It participated in the military exercises of the other paramilitary groups and later that year joined the *Reichsflagge* and *Oberland* in the German Military League (Schäfer, 1957, p. 7). By this reorganization, the SA was torn from Hitler's hands and became a tool of the army. Under the circumstances, there was little that Hitler could do—the party without the SA was inconceivable, and he could not afford to dissociate himself from it, but on the other hand, his dependence on the military prevented him from stopping Röhm's activities. Consequently, Hitler was forced to adopt a third alternative. In March, 1923, he called on Johann Klintsch to organize a personal guard which was to have absolute and exclusive loyalty to him. In May, 1923, this guard was made into the Stosstruppe Hitler, and its command was given to Josef Berchthold, a brawler rather than a professional military man (Heiden, 1944, p. 304; Bracher *et al.*, 1960, p. 837). It was out of this group that the SA was to develop after 1925.

The failure of the putsch of 1923 and the imprisonment of Hitler destroyed the party for all practical purposes. Although reorganization of the party had to wait until after Hitler's release from prison, the reorganization of the military side of the movement was started by Röhm in the spring of 1924. Before his arrest Hitler had granted unlimited powers to Röhm to rebuild the SA as the military arm of the party. Röhm, however, had other ideas. After his release from prison in April, 1924, he visited Hitler and outlined his plan to unite all military organizations under a single command. Hitler opposed the plan and declined to associate his name with Röhm's further activities (Röhm, 1928, pp. 289ff). As was to be expected, this did not sway Röhm from his course. In May he organized, independent of all party politics, the *Frontbann*, a military league dedicated to the military training of the "national-minded." Röhm's organizational talents were demonstrated by the rapid expansion of the Frontbann: by March, 1925, it had some thirty thousand men, including most of the völkisch military organization and the SA (Engelbrechten, 1940, pp. 33–34).

The Frontbann was intended to be an above-party cover organization and the military arm of the völkisch movement. As such it came under the nominal leadership of Ludendorff, who was at that time the unofficial head of the völkisch bloc. The dissensions within the bloc (see pp. 68–70), which became more pronounced after the Weimar congress of August, 1924, led Röhm to insist that the Frontbann be associated only with the völkisch idea, so it could survive the disrupting effects of the internal strife that was splitting the bloc into factions. As the prospects of unity within the völkisch bloc grew even dimmer toward the end of 1924, the Frontbann, if it were to maintain its unity, had to be made independent. But it was also imperative, for purposes of propaganda and recruitment, to preserve identification with the völkisch movement. Consequently, in November Röhm proposed that Hitler and Ludendorff, respectively, lead the political and the military parts of the movement (Röhm, 1928, pp. 295–297). Ludendorff, who by this time was hostile to anything that meant political association with Hitler, refused, and Hitler delayed his decison in order to keep all possibilities open (Röhm, 1928, pp. 307–308).

After Hitler's release from prison, the fate of the Frontbann was sealed. At the party conference on February 27, 1925, Hitler demanded that the Frontbann be joined to the NSDAP as a political instrument in the hands of party leadership.[20] Röhm refused, stubbornly adhering to the idea that the Frontbann had to be kept above politics as the military arm of the (nonexistent) national movement. The meeting of Frontbann leaders from February 28 to March 2 endorsed again the idea of two leaders, military and political, but the suggestion failed to elicit the support of either Hitler or Ludendorff (Röhm, 1928, pp. 308–309). Meanwhile, the directives from the local party leaders and from the Frontbann conflicted more often. Hitler and his subordinate party leaders demanded that Frontbann members obey their orders. When Hitler attempted to inflict disciplinary measures on Frontbann leaders, Röhm intervened, declaring that the Frontbann was not under Hitler's orders (Röhm, 1928, p. 312). The rupture was complete.

In April, 1925, Röhm made a last attempt at reconciliation. On April 16 he handed Hitler a memorandum in which he pointed out that the Frontbann was a success and that its thirty thousand men represented a national force which could be the foundation of a national political organization. He also appealed to their friendship and past association and asked for Hitler's confidence. He wanted Hitler to recognize his absolute authority over the Frontbann, without which neither discipline nor the successful organization, so aptly suited to carry the national idea all over Germany, could be maintained. Röhm knew that if he subordinated the Frontbann to the party, he would destroy everything that he had been working for since the spring of 1924 (Röhm, 1928, p. 313).

Hitler had no desire to make his party dependent on another organization. He was determined to follow through with his plans for the SA. He rejected Röhm's appeals and demanded the immediate subordination of the Frontbann to his authority. On April 17 Röhm asked Hitler to acknowledge his resignation from the Frontbann. Receiving no reply, he wrote a note to Hitler on April 30 tendering his resignation. His note was

[20] "Satzungen der National Sozialistische Deutsche Arbeiterpartei," Stanford University, Microfilm Collection, Reel 69, Folder 1509.

published in the Nazi press. Ludendorff wrote to him approving his decision; Hitler remained silent.[21] With Röhm's resignation and the collapse of the Frontbann, Hitler had a free hand to establish a new SA based on his own principles.[22]

THE QUESTION OF ELECTORAL ALLIANCES

Shortly before his arrest Hitler penciled a note to Alfred Rosenberg: "Dear Rosenberg: Lead the movement from now on" (Rosenberg, 1955, p. 107). Had Hitler possessed a sense of humor, this note might have been taken as a joke. There was no movement to speak of after November 9; its leaders were either arrested or in hiding, and what may have been left of its organization was outlawed. Under these circumstances Hitler called upon Rosenberg, whom he had never before consulted on organizational matters, to lead a nonexistent movement.[23] Rosenberg was the most ineffectual of all the Nazi leaders as an organizer and leader; he had no interest, no experience, and no talents in organization matters, no personal following, and only limited popularity. His arrogance did not sit well with the less educated, socially inferior members of the party leadership, and his preoccupation with theory made him ridiculous in the eyes of the more pragmatically minded military men. It is probable, however, that for Hitler these shortcomings were the best recommendations.

[21] Röhm, 1928, p. 316. It is interesting to note how Röhm failed to appreciate the nature of a totalitarian movement. The demand of absolute and exclusive loyalty which totalitarianism imposes upon its adherents was lost on him. This is illustrated by what he wrote in the Epilogue of his book: "I do not think that these three things are irreconcilable: (1) my loyalty to the House of Wittelsbach, (2) my admiration for Ludendorff, (3) my association with Hitler."

Röhm did not know where he failed Hitler; he thought himself innocent of any wrongdoing. In this he would have been correct had he dealt with a traditional instead of a totalitarian party leader.

[22] The Frontbann collapsed because its foundations were destroyed. The völkisch movement was dissolved and with it the justification for the Frontbann's existence was impaired. The era of international and domestic political crisis was temporarily superseded by the "era of fulfillment" and economic recovery. This weakened the sociological basis of the organization. Finally, the army, under the leadership of von Seeckt, refused to give its approval to the Frontbann idea. Hitler's action was merely the *coup de grâce*.

[23] "I was amazed," wrote Rosenberg in his memoirs, "for Hitler never consulted me on organizational matters before, and all of a sudden I was to take over in the most difficult times" (1955, p. 107).

The party, after November, 1923, lacked even the most rudimentary forms of unity and centralized leadership. Only local groups remained, usually estranged

The history of the movement[24] during Hitler's imprisonment is a confused maze of intrigues, plots, and alliances. The leadership of the party[25] was left without any political guidelines that might have prevented the intense intrigues and animosities that came to dominate relations in the upper echelons (Hanfstängl, 1957, pp. 108ff; Lüdecke, 1938, pp. 210ff). Every issue gave rise to intense conflicts among the leaders, none of whom acknowledged any authority in anyone else after Hitler had declared that nobody could speak in his name (Rosenberg, 1955, p. 110; Jochmann, 1963, pp. 78, 123).

The question that emerged immediately after the abortive putsch was about the attitude of the party toward the approaching elections in May, 1924. At the Salzburg meeting late in 1923, Albrecht von Graefe, leader of the Deutschvölkische Freiheitspartei, proposed to the leaders of the GVG the formation of a united bloc. The proposition sounded attractive to the majority of GVG leaders and was supported by Rosenberg for a variety of reasons. The völkisch movement offered an opportunity for the Nazis to extend their organization to North Germany, and hence the idea received the most enthusiastic support from the representatives of the northern districts. Their spokesman was Gregor Strasser, a southerner himself, but a man who recognized the potential of the party in the north. Association in a völkisch bloc seemed also to be the only opportunity for the party to participate in national politics—this was important for morale, prestige, and propaganda, and as a further benefit, it would increase the incomes of those elected (Rosenberg, 1955, p. 109).

For Hitler, however, the proposition did not seem so attractive. Graefe's offer meant continued dependence on others, especially dangerous at a time when the party was at the point of dissolution. Even more important to Hitler was the threat to himself that the offer posed. Being behind bars, he feared the loss of his authority, which he could now exercise only indirectly by delegation. The safest course for Hitler seemed to be to keep the party in suspended animation until he was free again to assume direct command over it. Consequently, when Rosenberg

from one another and without formal organizational ties. (Police Report, Stanford University, Microfilm Collection, Reel 68, Folder 1497A.)

[24] The party assumed the name of "Grossdeutsche Volksgemeinschaft" (GVG) to circumvent the prohibition. In literal translation: Great German Popular Community.

[25] In addition to Rosenberg's appointment, Hitler designated Max Amann as deputy leader and Hermann Esser and Julius Streicher as the other two members of the quadrumvirate (Hanfstängl, 1957, p. 108).

informed Hitler of Graefe's proposal and of the fact that Hitler's leadership of the bloc would not be accepted by the other parties, Hitler declared himself against it (Rosenberg, 1955, p. 109). Hitler's decision split the party into two groups. Some, led by Streicher and Esser (Lüdecke, 1938, pp. 219–221), loudly echoed Hitler's opposition and condemned joining the Graefe group. These people, mostly Bavarians, had assumed the leadership of the GVG with Hitler's blessing in January, 1924, and were to exhaust their energies during Hitler's imprisonment by personal quarrels; they were loyal adherents of Hitler (Lüdecke, 1938, pp. 248ff). The dissidents, led by Rosenberg and Gregor Strasser, joined the völkisch bloc and formed some months later the National Socialist Freedom Movement under the leadership of Graefe, Strasser, and Ludendorff (Strasser, 1948, p. 57; Schäfer, 1957, p. 7). Behind the aegis of the völkisch bloc, the organization-minded Strasser started to prepare for the future expansion of the party in the north (Strasser & Stern, 1943, p. 101).

The May, 1924, elections brought a minor triumph for the National Socialist Freedom Movement, which won some two million votes and captured thirty-two seats in the Reichstag (Frick, 1932, p. 37). Faced with a *fait accompli,* Hitler had to reverse himself and to approve the actions of those who acted in open defiance of his wishes (Lüdecke, 1938, p. 218). This blow to his authority taught Hitler a lesson he was not to forget; never again was he willing to identify himself with a position unless he knew that he had the power to make it prevail.[26] During the rest of his imprisonment Hitler remained aloof from party matters; he refused to make decisions or to voice opinions (Strasser, 1948, p. 58; Jochmann, 1963, pp. 78, 123).

In August the Weimar congress of the völkisch bloc was convened to map out a common strategy for the coming elections in December. Instead of furthering cohesion of the bloc, the congress showed signs that the bloc might dissolve (Röhm, 1928, p. 296). There were too many leaders and too many factions, and the völkisch idea itself was waning under the impact of economic recovery and stabilization of the international situation. In the December elections the National Socialist

[26] This was the real reason that Hitler resigned from the leadership of the party in 1924, not, as Alan Bullock contends, in order to appease the authorities (Bullock, 1959, p. 115). Hitler was quite explicit about this in the *Völkischer Beobachter* of February 26, 1925: "In mid-June, 1924, I had to abdicate my leadership because it was impossible for me to exercise real responsibility from prison."

Freedom Movement lost fifty per cent of its electoral support, and the number of its seats in the Reichstag fell to fourteen (Frick, 1932, p. 4).

Thereafter, the völkisch bloc and the National Socialist Freedom Movement rapidly declined. On December 20, 1924, Hitler was released from prison, and in February of the following year the Nazis, under the leadership of Gregor Strasser, left the National Socialist Freedom Movement. Later others followed them into the ranks of the newly organized NSDAP (National Socialist German Workers' Party). By 1928 the National Socialist Freedom Movement disappeared, leaving the NSDAP the only nation-wide political organization claiming the heritage of the völkisch idea (Frick, 1932, pp. 4–5).

卐   卐   卐

The common denominator in these three conflicts is the idea of a totalitarian organization. Each of these instances promulgated some principle of a totalitarian party. In 1921 the principle of absolute leadership was questioned by the old guard; in 1924 the National Socialist Freedom Movement contradicted by its existence the principle of exclusiveness; the problem of the SA involved both. Hitler was consistently on the totalitarian side, even though he had not yet developed his ideas about a totalitarian organization systematically. Owing to the shortcomings of his political organization, he suffered defeats or won only incomplete and temporary victories.

The factional conflicts of the later period were to raise some of the same questions, but devolved in a different political context. By the time he had served his sentence, Hitler had outgrown his putschism. During 1925 and 1926 he set out to reorganize the party on totalitarian principles that were to affect the nature of intraparty conflicts. The party after 1925 acquired a broad membership, a Weltanschauung, and a charismatic leader. These features could not fail to have some effects on factional conflicts.

VI

The Northern Factions, 1925–1930

THE year 1924 marks the passing of a distinct phase of National Socialism. Before that date the movement was regional, restricted largely to Bavaria and to the southern part of Germany. Politically, it was strongly identified with the nationalism of the forces of the right and the military; its propaganda and organizational activities were predicated on the idea of a putsch.[1] Beginning with 1924 emphasis in each of these concerns of the party shifted considerably. As a result of Gregor Strasser's organizational talents and his alliances with the völkisch groups of North Germany, National Socialism made considerable headway in the north after 1924 (see Table 1).

The number of local party organizations in the south declined because of the problems inherent in Hitler's determination to organize a new party out of the remnants of the old. The functioning local party organizations were informed early in March, 1925, that as of that moment old membership cards were invalid and that everyone had to submit new applications for membership to the headquarters in Munich.[2] This created grave problems for the local party leaders, who found it difficult to make members of the old party understand why they should pay new initiation fees.[3] Other local difficulties arose from Hit-

---

[1] The obsolescence of putschist tactics had already been pointed out by Feder in August, 1923. In his letter of August 10, he urged Hitler to pay greater attention to organizational matters. "The times of the condottieri have passed," he warned. (Hale, 1958, p. 359.)

[2] See the correspondence of Philip Bouhler (party business manager) with local party leaders in National Archives, *German Documents*, Reels 20–26.

[3] The party correspondence provides ample evidence for this. See, for instance,

Table 1. The Development of Local Party Organizations,
1923–1925

Districts	No. of Local Organizations	
	1923	1925
Southern		
Bavarian eastern frontier	75	57
Upper Bavaria	22	16
Württemberg-Hohenzollern	37	20
Swabia	32	16
Lower Franconia	24	13
Franconia	22	18
Northern		
Düsseldorf	10	20
Essen	3	9
Berlin	1	9
Kassel	5	15
Mecklenburg	0	14
East Hanover	0	11
Pomerania	3	10
Saxony	27	88
South Hanover	8	40
Thuringia	14	46

SOURCE: Wolfgang Schäfer, *NSDAP: Entwicklung und Struktur der Staatspartei des dritten Reiches* (Hanover & Frankfort on the Main: Norddeutsche, O. Goedel, 1957), p. 11. Used with permission of the publisher.

ler's demand that local party organizations rupture their ties with all völkisch groups and that no party member simultaneously belong to any völkisch association.[4] This was a bitter pill for many local party leaders who had traditionally identified the Nazi party with the völkisch idea, and many refused to make the break and to subordinate themselves unconditionally to Hitler's leadership. As a consequence of these factors, several local party organizations seceded or were dissolved in the early months of 1925, especially in the southern areas where most of the Nazi party organizations existed before 1925.[5] In the north most

the letter of the district leader of Lüneburg-Stade to Bouhler, dated May 15, 1925. National Archives, *German Documents*, Reel 21.

[4] See Hitler's "Summons to the Former Members of the NSDAP," and "The Fundamental Directives Relating to the Re-establishment of the NSDAP," in *Völkischer Beobachter*, February 26, 1925.

[5] Hitler's tactics toward the dissident local party leaders varied according to the local circumstances. Some he dismissed outright by dissolving their local organizations; in other instances he merged several local organizations and thereby forced the dissident leaders to bow to the will of the majority of their followers. See, for

of the local organizations were being built from the bottom up; hence, that area was not correspondingly affected by these problems.

However (fortunately for Hitler), because of the organizational weakness of the völkisch movement, most of the dissident Nazi leaders were forced to the realization in the following months or years that they had no future outside the Hitler party. Soon they were to bow to Hitler's point of view, one by one capitulating unconditionally to his demands.[6] Thus, the decline of the local party organizations in the south was only a temporary phenomenon; by 1928 they had overcome their setback of 1925 (Table 2).

Table 2. The Development of Local Party Organizations, 1925–1928

Districts	No. of Local Organizations	
	1925	1928
Southern		
Baden	31	62
Bavarian eastern frontier	57	115
Franconia	18	36
Upper Bavaria	16	32
Northern		
Düsseldorf	20	21
Essen	9	11
Berlin	9	28

SOURCE: Wolfgang Schäfer, *NSDAP: Entwicklung und Struktur der Staatspartei des dritten Reiches* (Hanover & Frankfort on the Main: Norddeutsche, O. Goedel, 1957), p. 12. Used with permission of the publisher.

It is important to note that although they were impressive on paper, these shifts did not represent any corresponding shifts in the real balance of party power in the south and the north. Although the northern districts underwent a period of relative stagnation in membership in the late 1920's, for some time after 1925 they still remained the most promising part of the movement (Lüdecke, 1938, p. 341). Their promise lay in their attempts to identify themselves with the working classes,

example, the Württemberg case in the Bavarian Police Reports, Stanford University, Microfilm Collection, Reel 70, Folder 1515; and the Cologne district reports in National Archives, *German Documents*, Reel 21.

[6] See Professor Mergenthaler's capitulation to Hitler in June, 1927. Stanford University, Microfilm Collection, Reel 70, Folder 1515.

whereas the southern districts still clung for the most part to the bourgeois, antisocialist, racist idea of National Socialism.[7] Munich remained the business and spiritual stronghold of the movement, but there was little question that the dynamic part of the organization lay in the north.

THE WORKING ASSOCIATION OF THE NORTH AND WEST

The socialistic, working-class orientation of the movement in the north after 1925 cannot be conclusively supported by the available statistical data.[8] However, ample persuasive evidence to this effect can be gathered from the accessible party correspondence for 1925–1926. In their frequent (almost daily) reports to headquarters, the local party leaders of the north stressed the importance of associating their movement with the left in order to attract members of the working classes.[9] Thus, the local leader of the city of Lübeck stressed the importance of "going to the workers." "If we can get only fifty Social Democrats," he asserted, "we are better off and are more secure than if we had a battalion of the Tannenberg League with seven officers and sixty men." In conclusion he affirmed that "Playing soldiers won't help here."[10] District leader Klant of Hamburg reported to headquarters: "We have won fifty workers, which pleases us more than fifty doctors."[11] Reports from

[7] National Socialism in Bavaria remained basically a lower-middle-class affair closely allied with the forces of the right. The typical concerns of Bavarian local party meetings in the 1920's were the Jews, international capital, and religion. See Joseph Goebbels's remark in Semmler, 1947, pp. 56–57; Hitler, 1953, p. 67; police reports on the meetings of the Ansbach local organization, Stanford University, Microfilm Collection, Reel 5, Folder 134.

[8] Only fragmentary lists of members are available. The files of the Berlin Document Center (National Archives) contain initial membership lists for only seven districts comprising a total of about two hundred members. Roughly, about one third of them can be classified as workers; the rest were members of the middle classes, students, and professionals. Their average age in 1925 was twenty-nine years. See National Archives, *German Documents,* Reels 20–26.

[9] In some districts this had been achieved to such an extent that the Nazis were regarded as standing shoulder to shoulder with the Communists on economic matters (report from Danzig, March 20, 1926, National Archives, *German Documents,* Reel 20). In other districts the leaders warned against identification with the right (report from Hamburg, November 11, 1925, *ibid.,* Reel 21; report from East Hanover, January 29, 1926, *ibid.,* Reel 21).

The Berlin Nazis called themselves "Hitlerproleten," or Hitler's proletariat, thus indicating their socialistic, lower-class origins and orientations (Reinhold Muchow's report from Berlin, August, 1926, in Stanford University, Microfilm Collection, Reel 5, Folder 133).

[10] National Archives, *German Documents,* report from Lübeck, December 14, 1925, Reel 23.

[11] *Ibid.,* report from Hamburg, March 24, 1925, Reel 20.

Danzig,[12] Halle,[13] East Hanover,[14] South Hanover,[15] Elbe-Havel district,[16] Anhalt-Dessau,[17] Mecklenburg,[18] and Schleswig-Holstein[19] contained similar sentiments and listed with great pride and self-satisfaction the party's successes in industrial districts. Many of these districts suggested the formation of National Socialist trade unions to attract more manual workers.[20]

Thus the socialist element became a prominent part of Nazi appeals in the north after 1924. Social justice, nationalization of the economy, "bread community," and other socialistic tenets were prominent in the speeches of Gregor Strasser.[21] That these principles were not ends in themselves but means to the establishment of an organic national community was of crucial significance, but a distinction too subtle to be noticed by those to whom the speeches were addressed. (The socialism of the northerners was basically the socialism of the small bourgeoisie (Kühnl, 1966, p. 322).) What was important for Strasser's audiences was the emphasis on these principles; for what ends they were to be used was of secondary importance.

The post-1924 tendencies in the north introduced significant changes in the organizational base of the movement. The keystones of the northern part of the movement were the local organizations that local citizens initiated and financed with membership dues and private contributions.[22] The network of local organizations put the movement on a more secure foundation and was important during the relative economic prosperity and international peace of the late 1920's. These local cells be-

---

[12] *Ibid.*, reports of October 6, 1925, and January 15, 1926, Reel 20.

[13] *Ibid.*, report of October 11, 1926, Reel 20.

[14] *Ibid.*, Telschow to Goebbels October 23, 1925, Reel 21.

[15] *Ibid.*, report of May 15, 1925, Reel 21.

[16] *Ibid.*, reports of December 18 and 27, 1925; February, 1926, Reel 22.

[17] *Ibid.*, report of November 3, 1925, Reel 22.

[18] *Ibid.*, reports of April 8, June 18, and December 14, 1925, Reel 23.

[19] *Ibid.*, reports of March 1 and May 5, 1925, Reel 25.

[20] The party headquarters was besieged by local organizations for directions on the subject of trade unions, but their pleas remained unanswered. "The trade union question is under consideration and is to be decided shortly" was Bouhler's usual reply. See reports from Elbe-Havel district for February, 1926, National Archives, *German Documents*, Reel 22; from Danzig, January 15, 1926, Reel 20; Anhalt-Dessau, November 3, 1925, Reel 22; and Bouhler's replies on succeeding dates.

[21] See the collection of Gregor Strasser's speeches in his books, *Freiheit und Brot* (n.d.) and *Kampf um Deutschland* (1932).

[22] Abel, 1938, pp. 78–81; Krebs, 1959, p. 41. Not only did the local organizations not receive any help from Munich, but they were required to send to Munich a substantial portion of their hard-earned funds. See more on this below, pp. 77–79.

came indispensable nuclei around which the great masses of new party members were organized after 1929. These changes were by no means contrary to the ideas that Hitler had developed in prison. Indeed, they implemented those concepts of the party laid down in *Mein Kampf*: the necessity for a broad popular base, dissociation from the right-wing bourgeois forces, and systematic party organization on the principle of absolute leadership.[23] What produced the differences between the northerners and Hitler was the principle of absolute leadership and questions of tactics, not basic issues of substance (Jochmann, 1963, pp. 207ff).

On his release from prison in 1924, Hitler set out to forge a strongly disciplined party from the loose association of local organizations, all that remained of the old party.[24] At that time there was no effective central leadership in Munich, and the local organizations, left to their own devices for so long, had begun to develop independent attitudes. Many entered into close relations with other groups, völkisch or socialist (depending on the local circumstances), without bothering to keep Munich informed about their activities. Meanwhile corresponding confusion reigned in Munich. Esser, Feder, Rosenberg, Bouhler, and Schwarz met in Munich but had little more in common than their physical proximity. Gregor Strasser spent most of his time in Berlin or traveling around North Germany trying to organize Nazism there.[25] Röhm was busy with his Frontbann activities and seemed to care little about the politicians' problems.

In the first issue of the new *Völkischer Beobachter* (February 26, 1925), Hitler published his "Fundamental Directives" for the new party, and on the next day he convened his first party meeting in Munich. On this public occasion he appealed to all Nazis to bury their differences[26]

[23] During his imprisonment, and in the years immediately following his release from Landsberg, Hitler was bitterly opposed to the bourgeoisie. He blamed the bourgeoisie and the bourgeois spirit for the failure of the November putsch. This contempt comes forth with particular intensity in the pages of *Mein Kampf* and was also evident in his speeches of this period. See Hitler, 1939, pp. 59, 225, 567, 612; Stanford University, Microfilm Collection, Reel 70, Folder 1515.

[24] On the character of the Nazi party in 1924 see Munich Police Report, Stanford University, Microfilm Collection, Reel 68, Folder 1497A.

[25] The task of reconstruction of the party organization in North Germany was given to Gregor Strasser by Hitler on March 11, 1925 (Kühnl, 1966, p. 318).

[26] Hitler's motto throughout the "years of fighting" was "let bygones be bygones." As he stated in the first issue of the *Völkischer Beobachter*, the first and overriding task of the leader was to achieve unity in the party.

and to unite behind him for the sake of the movement. According to one observer, the result verged on the ridiculous: "Singly and in pairs, men who had been bitter enemies mounted the platform and shook hands, some of them unable to restrain the tears which Hitler's magic voice had worked up. In groups they vowed their forgiveness of each other and swore undying loyalty to the Führer."[27]

The unity of February, 1925, remained confined to the leadership of the party for several months to come[28]—it took Hitler and Bouhler that long to bring the majority of the independent local leaders into line and impose on them unitary party discipline. The party of 1925 was anything but disciplined and well organized. Conflicting sets of local leaders competed for recognition in numerous districts, and it was sometimes difficult for those sitting in Munich to know which faction would turn out to be more trustworthy in the future.[29] By the end of the year, however, most of the local leaders had got official recognition, and the central authority of Munich was beginning to be effectively exerted on the local levels.

As a consequence of cleverly designed policies, the central office in Munich under the effective direction of its business manager, Philip Bouhler, successfully extended its supervision and control over the minute details of local and district party organizations.[30] The exclusive right of the central office to issue membership cards enabled it to keep accurate accounts of party membership in each district. Since the num-

[27] Lüdecke, 1938, p. 258. See also Munich Police Reports, Stanford University, Microfilm Collection, Reel 69, Folder 1509, and Reel 87, Folder 1835. Three important party personalities were absent from this meeting, but two of them responded favorably to Hitler's appeal for unity. Gregor Strasser and Rosenberg accepted the new party principles, but Röhm refused to accede to Hitler's wish to subordinate the Frontbann to the party. He resigned from his offices two months later.

[28] The unity was more apparent than real even on the highest levels. The mortal enemies of 1924 were friends in 1925 only on public occasions and in the presence of Hitler. Personality conflicts and rivalries continued, but since they did not affect Hitler's leadership, they were allowed to persist. See Hermann Fobke's report in Jochmann, 1963, pp. 207ff.

[29] Conflicts were particularly noticeable in Berlin during the summer of 1926, National Archives, German Documents, Reel 19; Halle during the summer of 1925 through the summer of 1926, ibid., Reel 20; Hamburg in the spring of 1926, ibid., Reel 21; South Rhineland in the spring of 1925, ibid., Reel 22; and in East Prussia in the spring of 1925, ibid., Reel 24.

[30] During 1925 and 1926 many local organizations were directly subordinated to Munich pending the establishment of district organizational nomenclature at this time.

ber of members determined the financial obligations of the local organizations to Munich, this knowledge enabled Bouhler to exercise strict control over local party finances. Local party organizations were required to collect one reichsmark for each new member and fifty pfennigs each month thereafter. The initiation fees and half of the monthly membership dues were to be forwarded by the local organizations to the district offices if these existed, otherwise directly to Munich. The district party leaders were also required to forward to Munich the initiation fees and ten pfennigs of each member's monthly dues. In addition, all extra contributions that local and district party leaders may have received from private citizens or groups were to be sent intact to Munich.[31]

It is easy to appreciate how many local party leaders began to resent the progressive imposition of such central controls and supervision. The delays in the issuance of membership cards exasperated local leaders, who found themselves besieged by applicants who demanded their cards upon paying their fees. Such local difficulties did not seem to have impressed the people in Munich, who adamantly insisted on the scrupulous examination of each application, regardless of the delay. However, delays were the lesser problem from the local point of view. The real source of irritation was the financial obligation imposed by Munich on the district and local party organizations. Regardless of local circumstances, Bouhler demanded one reichsmark for each new applicant and ten pfennigs each month for every registered member. Local party leaders argued that many of their members were unemployed workers, students, old people, or disabled veterans who did not have the money to pay; Bouhler was unimpressed and answered by monotonously repeating the official regulations and reminding the local leaders that their situation was not unique but shared by most of the other local organizations. In order to extract the money due to Munich, Bouhler frequently went so far as to refuse to issue new membership cards for the local districts or to send speakers there until financial affairs had been straightened out. This was of great importance for the local leaders, who depended on Munich for literate speakers. The big prize here, of course, was Hitler, and Bouhler duly recognized this when he de-

[31] See these requirements as stated in Bouhler's letter to district leader Ernst in Halle, September 25, 1925, National Archives, *German Documents*, Reel 20.

clared on one occasion that Hitler would not visit districts that owed money to Munich.[32]

Some exasperated local leaders, Goebbels and Kaufmann among them,[33] issued their own membership cards in open defiance of party regulations. When called to account by Bouhler, they defiantly admitted their action. They accused Bouhler of having no idea of local party affairs and declared with amazing audacity that they had yet to see the contributions of the headquarters in Munich to the development of the movement. They argued that it was impossible to require old Nazis to pay another initiation fee, especially when many of them had spent time in prison for having been Nazis, and that, similarly, it was impossible to collect dues from the unemployed.[34] These sentiments were more typical than unusual and were rooted in the attitudes of the man in the field toward the members of the general staff. There was widespread belief among local leaders that whereas they were carrying the lion's share of the work, the headquarters got the lion's share of the dues. There were dissatisfactions with the inefficiency of the Munich office as well as with occasionally conflicting directives from Munich.[35]

Such dissatisfactions on the local level were aggravated in the north by the perceptible differences in orientations between the north and the Munich leadership.[36] By the summer of 1925 preparations for an offen-

[32] Bouhler to the Nuremberg local, July 26, 1926, National Archives, *German Documents*, Reel 20.

[33] District leaders Rust (Hanover), Fobke (Göttingen), Schultz (Hesse-Nassau-North), and Lohse (Schleswig-Holstein) proposed in a joint letter to Bouhler (April 15, 1925) that membership cards be issued by district leaders in order to save time and paperwork and to escape the problem of undue centralization. (National Archives, *German Documents*, Reel 21.)

[34] Correspondence North Rhineland district, October 22, 1925, National Archives, *German Documents*, Reel 22.

[35] Ernst (Halle district) to Hess, September, 1925: "there seem to be two orders, one from you and one from the party office. Which should be followed?" (National Archives, *German Documents*, Reel 20).

Josef Klant (Hamburg district) to Bouhler (March 21, 1925): "No answer from Headquarters, no membership books, no application forms, no *Völkischer Beobachter*. Even Hitler's personality cannot make good what the organization ruins." (Jochmann, 1963, p. 207.)

[36] The presidential elections of March–April, 1925, exhibited these differences when, after much vacillation, Hitler decided to support Hindenburg on the second ballot. Hitler's action associated the party with the monarchist, conservative-völkisch groups of Graefe and constituted a serious embarrassment for the northerners, who were aligned with Ludendorff's Tannenberg League—a völkisch, anti-capitalistic organization. See the *Völkischer Beobachter* of March 14, March 21, and April 10, 1925, and Lüdecke, 1938, p. 264; Miltenberg, 1931, p. 64; Strasser, 1948, p. 81.

sive against the "reactionary-bureaucratic" elements in Munich and against the "ruinous Munich course" were noticeable in the North (Jochmann, 1963, pp. 207–211). Goebbels's diary entries for August 15, 16, and 19 hint at great things to come in September (Heiber, n.d., pp. 20–21). Sentiments for some concerted action to oppose Esser's dictatorship grew sharper among northern party leaders.

The first meeting of the northerners took place in Hagen, Westphalia, on September 10, 1925, at the invitation of Gregor Strasser. Although Strasser himself could not be present, the meeting was attended by almost all district leaders from Prussia (except for Berlin, East Prussia, Silesia, and Hesse). The participants endorsed a Working Association of the North and West districts, which was to further greater unity in organization and propaganda, exchange of speakers and, if necessary, a common program toward day-to-day questions. The *National Socialist Letters* (*Nationalsozialistische Briefe*) edited by Goebbels appeared on October 1 as the mouthpiece of the Association (Jochmann, 1963, pp. 207–219; Kühnl, 1966, p. 320).

By the end of the year the North represented a fairly unified organization against the Esser machine in Munich. At their second meeting, on November 22, the association came to open revolt against the party organization in Munich. Gregor Strasser presented his programmatic ideas and Goebbels and Kaufmann were delegated to draft a broader program for the next meeting, to be held in January (Kühnl, 1966, p. 320).

Much has been made of this program and of the Hanover conference of January 25, 1926. It has been alleged that this movement was secessionist, was primarily ideologically oriented, and was directed against Hitler's leadership (see Bullock, 1959, pp. 120ff; Görlitz & Quint, 1952, pp. 256ff; Heiden, 1935, pp. 113ff; *id*, 1944, pp. 286ff; and the books by Otto Strasser). However, the party correspondence of the period tends to refute such interpretations and so do contemporary diaries and documents. Available primary sources show persuasively that the northern districts never developed into a separate party, but worked under effective control throughout the period (see pp. 77ff). Contemporary documents also reveal that the programmatic division between north and south was not so sharp as it has usually been portrayed.[37] It can also be shown that although several of these leaders resented the firm hand

[37] Had the programmatic division been as sharp as some writers maintain, there would hardly have been such demand on the part of northern leaders to have Esser,

of Bouhler, nothing was further from their minds than challenging Hitler's leadership. Hitler remained the only concrete point of unity in the heterogeneous movement. He was above the conflicts, and he was regarded "as something mystical, unreal."[38]

On January 25, 1926, the Hanover meeting was convened. At this important meeting twenty-four northern party leaders represented seven northern party districts. The congress resolved to organize the Working Association of the North and West, elected its officers, approved its propaganda organ, and adopted the draft program. The unanimity of the congress was broken only by Feder and Robert Ley.[39]

The conference elected Gregor Strasser the leader of the Association, elected Otto Strasser its propaganda chief and editor of the *National Socialist Letters*, and appointed Goebbels editorial writer. The editorial offices and the press of the Association were to be known thereafter as the Kampfverlag.[40]

The program of the Association was by no means a radical departure from the party program of 1920. Indeed Kühnl is correct in saying that the program was designed more to keep Munich to the original twenty-five points, than to revise the 1920 program (1966, p. 322). Little is known about the proceedings of the conference. According to Otto Strasser, sentiments were expressed against the absolute authority of the leader. "We acknowledge no Pope who can claim infallibility," Bernhard Rust is reported to have exclaimed (Strasser & Stern, 1943, pp. 115–116). Such exclamations, however, assuming that they really were made, should not obscure the crucial fact that the meeting was not directed against Hitler, but was organized to impress upon him the necessity of holding to the original party program and preventing the progressive dilution of its socialistic tenets. The conference did not repudiate Hitler's leadership but sought to capture his charismatic symbol for

Rosenberg, Streicher, and other representatives of the south as speakers in their districts. Nor would the southern districts have been so keen on having Gregor Strasser speak at their meetings. National Archives, *German Documents,* Reels 19–26; Kühnl, 1966, pp. 321ff.

[38] Görlitz & Quint, 1952, p. 253. According to Goebbels, it was in Hitler's presence that Strasser and he decided to draft a new program (Heiber, n.d., p. 43).

[39] Feder was the twenty-fifth member of the congress. He was an outsider who had been sent by Hitler to observe the proceedings. The accounts of this meeting are fragmentary. See Strasser & Stern, 1943, pp. 115ff; Heiber, n.d., pp. 55–56; Miltenberg, 1931, p. 70; Heiden, 1935, p. 287; Görlitz & Quint, 1952, p. 257.

[40] The word "Kampfverlag" literally means "Publishing House of the Battle." The term was to reflect the revolutionary sentiments of its founders.

their cause. That this may have been their mistake was argued by Otto Strasser at a later date: "Perhaps we should have acted at that moment, made Hitler honorary president and thus prevented him from doing any damage by depriving him of all effective power in the party. We did nothing because we thought ourselves to be much more powerful than he. This was our error and it must be recognized." (Strasser, 1941, p. 189.)

However, Strasser distorted the circumstances of 1925. The reason they did not depose Hitler was not that they overestimated their power, but that they knew that without Hitler the party could not survive. They needed Hitler's name and authority. Besides, if they had wanted to get rid of Hitler, they should have done so in December or January, before Hitler had re-established his authority. At that time Gregor Strasser decided for Hitler and gave up the last chance to continue without him. The point is that they did not think of getting rid of him—on the contrary, they thought him to be on their side, and they were sure that they would capture him for their positions, as Goebbels's diary makes clear.[41]

The Hanover meeting of January, 1926, brought into the open the disagreements between the two camps. What made Hitler intervene and summon the Bamberg conference for February 14 were not the programmatic disagreements, which had existed for some time (and which were to continue), but the direct challenge that the Hanover conference implied to the principle of absolute leadership.

Many of the accounts published about the Bamberg conference can safely be classified as fiction. They have not only misrepresented the ascertainable facts about the conference, but have been predicated on the mistaken assumption that the Bamberg meeting was called to put an end to the Association which was organized against Hitler. A representative account may be quoted from the most authoritative study on the history of Nazism: "On 14 February, 1926, he [Hitler] summoned a conference in his turn, this time in the South German town of Bamberg. Hitler deliberately avoided a Sunday, when the North German

---

[41] "We shall put on a nice act in Bamberg and shall win over Hitler," wrote Goebbels in his diary on February 11, 1926 (Heiber, n.d., p. 59). It seems now fairly certain that Goebbels never expressed the wish at that conference that Hitler should be expelled from the party, as reported by Strasser & Stern, 1943, pp. 115–116. His diaries manifest his unwavering support and loyalty to Hitler.

Fobke reports that several dissident Nazi groups were formed under the motto, "With Hitler, without Esser" (Jochmann, 1963, p. 207).

leaders would have been free to attend in strength. As a result, the Strasser wing of the Party was represented only by Gregor Strasser and Goebbels." (Bullock, 1959, pp. 122–123; see also Heiden, 1935, pp. 287–289; Olden, 1936, pp. 202–203; Strasser, 1941, pp. 191–203, 1948, pp. 88–91, 100–101; Strasser & Stern, 1943, pp. 121–123.)

In contrast to such accounts, the contemporary police report shows that the meeting was held on Sunday (which was on February 14), and was attended by sixty to sixty-five party leaders. Several of these were from the north: Schlange (Berlin), Ernst (Halle), Hindenbrand (Mecklenburg), Glans (Hamburg), Rust (Hanover), and Strasser and Goebbels.[42] It is not known how many other northern party leaders were present, since the police report does not include a complete list of the participants, but it is obvious that several of the most important leaders from the north were able to attend.[43]

In the absence of documentary evidence, the rest of the speculation in the quotation above from Bullock cannot be challenged with equal certainty. It can be argued, however, that the site of the conference was not chosen in order to make the cost of travel prohibitive for northern leaders. Had this been Hitler's intention, the logical site would have been Munich, some hundred and fifty miles further south. Indeed, it may be argued that it was in Hitler's interest to have as many northerners at the meeting as possible.[44] Hitler's purpose for calling the Bamberg conference was not to defeat the northern leaders, but to convince them of the necessity for party unity. He did not regard the northerners as his opponents but as subordinates who had to be brought back to the right track. Besides, Nazi party meetings were not called to make decisions

[42] Stanford University, Microfilm Collection, Reel 33A, Folder 1788. The meeting on February 14 was secret; no party members other than leaders were allowed to attend. The next day there was a public meeting of six to seven hundred persons at which the agreements reached at the secret meeting were publicly announced.

[43] It can be seen from the party correspondence that more leaders were invited from the north than were actually present. District leaders Fobke (South Hanover–Braunschweig) and Viereck (Elbe-Havel) declined the invitation. (National Archives, *German Documents*, Fobke's letter to Hess, February 2, 1926, Reel 21; Viereck's letter to Bouhler, February 11, 1926, Reel 23.) Although most party leaders received invitations, some did not. Kaufmann (South Rhineland) complained to Bouhler that he had not received an invitation, although to his knowledge everybody else had. Bouhler informed him that not all district leaders had been invited. (*Ibid.*, Reel 22.)

[44] "Bamberg was chosen as the site of the conference in order to enable those living far away to come" (Bouhler's correspondence to Viereck, February 9, 1926, National Archives, *German Documents*, Reel 22).

by majority rule, and thus, the number of northern leaders present was quite irrelevant to the outcome of the conference. To maintain that the reason for Hitler's "victory" at Bamberg was a packed conference reveals a basic misunderstanding of Hitler's relation with the northern leaders and also of the nature of decision-making in the Nazi party.

There are no known official records of the proceedings of the conference.[45] The account which appeared in the official party newspaper indicates clearly enough, however, the major points of Hitler's concern. According to the *Völkischer Beobachter* (February 25, 1926), Hitler addressed himself to three main topics. First, he rejected Strasser's idea of a Russian entente that, according to Hitler, would have meant the bolshevization of Germany. Instead, he suggested that British and Italian alliances offered the most promising possibilities for Germany. He regarded the east as an area of colonization. (The idea of the Russian entente was not part of the program (see Kühnl, 1966, pp. 324–333).) Secondly, he rejected the northerners' position with respect to the expropriation of royal properties on the principle that "nothing should be given to them [princes] which does not belong to them," but also that nothing should be taken away from them which belongs to them. "We are for rights," he declared. "We know only Germans, not princes." Thirdly, he prohibited anyone from raising religious issues in the party because these "have no place in National Socialism."

This is the extent of the newspaper's report of the meeting. It ends: "The rest of the meeting was taken up by programmatic discussions in which several people participated besides Hitler, especially Feder, Strasser and Streicher. Complete agreement was achieved."

Otto Strasser's account goes beyond this report and states that the conference adopted the following resolutions: (1) abandonment of the Hanover program and reaffirmation of the twenty-five points; (2) dissolution of the Association and the establishment of unified party organization; (3) nomination of all district leaders by Hitler; (4) creation of a party tribunal to regulate intraparty disputes, with the power to expel members and to dissolve local organizations: the members of this tribunal were to be nominated by Hitler; and (5) establishment of the SA (1941, p. 193).

---

[45] "There is no agenda for the Conference. Hitler wants to discuss a series of important questions." (Bouhler's letter to Viereck, February 6, 1926, National Archives, *German Documents*, Reel 22.)

The outcome of the conference is generally referred to as a victory for Hitler. I submit that this is a misinterpretation, since there existed no movement against Hitler. At the conference Hitler refused to go along with the northern point of view, and this was a great blow to Strasser and Goebbels.[46] However, Hitler did not handle them as defeated enemies; although the Association had to be dissolved, its propaganda organ in Berlin was allowed to continue. Gregor Strasser was put in charge of party propaganda, and just a few months later Goebbels was named district leader in Berlin-Brandenburg.[47]

The decisions of the conference proved conclusive. The Working Association of the North and West was immediately dissolved;[48] Gregor Strasser went to Munich to assume his new position, continuing his association with his brother in the Kampfverlag. If the northern Association had been directed against Hitler, the decision of a "packed" conference would not have been accepted as a matter of course, but in fact, there was not a single resignation or expulsion. Herbert Blank's argument that the district leaders and Gregor Strasser abided by Hitler's decision in early 1926 because they were financially dependent on their party offices is not convincing; four years later this may have been a more important factor (Miltenberg, 1931, pp. 78–79).

The readiness with which Hitler's decisions were followed by the northern leaders, who only two weeks before had manifested such remarkable unity and strength of conviction in adopting their draft program and founding their Association, is not puzzling if one recognizes that their actions had not been directed against Hitler, but were predicated on his support. When Hitler pronounced the Hanover program wrong, the northerners, disappointed as they were, accepted his verdict.

[46] See Goebbels's entry in his diary for February 15, 1926, in Heiber, n.d., pp. 59–61.

[47] It is not true that Goebbels deserted Gregor Strasser at the conference, as was reported by Otto Strasser and repeated by others. It was not until several weeks later that Goebbels was offered and accepted the district leadership in Berlin. On March 26 he notes in his diary the receipt of Hitler's letter and the invitation to speak in Munich, which he eagerly accepted (Heiber, n.d., p. 68). For Otto Strasser's accounts, see 1948, p. 90; Strasser & Stern, 1943, pp. 122–123. Otto Strasser has since admitted that his early accounts of Goebbels's treason were exaggerated (Manvell & Fraenkel, 1960, p. 287).

[48] The Working Association of the North and West was dissolved when its Hanover program was repudiated by Hitler. On March 5, 1926, Gregor Strasser sent a memorandum to the members of the Working Association requesting the return of the Strasser program. The returned programs were probably then destroyed (Kühnl, 1966, p. 323).

It is important to note, however, that Hitler did not attack the substance of the Hanover program. Indeed, his factotum Goebbels, whom he had sent to Berlin in late 1926, assumed a position just as socialistic and anti-capitalistic as that of the other northern leaders. Programmatic heterogeneity was a characteristic of the Nazi movement from its inception; it was of no concern to Hitler. There was no Nazi ideology that would have required uniformity and orthodoxy; there was only a Weltanschauung, whose only orthodoxy was the totalitarian principle of absolute obedience to an absolute leader.

Hitler called the Bamberg conference to ward off possible threats to his leadership. The quasi-independent organization of the northern districts implicitly challenged the Nazi principle that the leader was the sole center of the movement and that no other institution or body of persons was to have an all-encompassing competence or any authorities except those delegated by the leader. The Hanover conference challenged this principle by assuming the right to decide questions pertinent to the movement as a whole, a right reserved to Hitler. That the conference meant only to guide Hitler back to the true path was immaterial to the issue.

The second threat to Hitler's absolute leadership was the proposed party program adopted in Hanover. Again, it was not the substance of the program that was important, but the mere existence of it. A program which is more than an opportunistic tool in the hands of the leader is by definition incompatible with absolute leadership. Such a program becomes organically related to the goals of the movement and thus becomes ideological; as such, it binds the leader to certain courses of action and may be used as a standard to evaluate the leader's actions. An ideological program gives every member of the political party an opportunity (if not an obligation) to judge the actions of the leader and to call him to account. The leader becomes an executive and ceases to be a "philosopher"; his responsibility will be to implement rather than to formulate the principles of the program.

It is not certain to what extent the members of the Hanover conference were aware of these implications of their actions. Certainly, the idea of a democratic party organization was far removed from their minds. Their concern was simple and immediate: they wanted to set down the "true" principles of Nazism, or, rather, those which promised the greatest political success. They did not think that these principles would be necessarily incompatible with the idea of absolute leadership, which they understood only imperfectly. The participants in the Hanover conference did not mean to challenge Hitler's authority; they only meant to fight the people who surrounded Hitler in Munich. It was a conflict between the men in the field and the courtiers of the party headquarters. The Hanoverians were not aware, as Hitler was, of the implications of their resolutions on the principles of charismatic authority. Had they been aware that they were challenging Hitler's authority, they would hardly have counted on his support in Bamberg.

Again, all this was immaterial from Hitler's point of view, for he realized immediately the implications of the draft program. At the Bamberg conference Hitler rejected the Hanover program; in May he declared the 1920 program unalterable (Volz, 1934, p. 14). This placed all discussion about the program out of order, and the party took another step toward totalitarianism.

The aim of the founders of the Working Association of the North and West from 1925 to 1926 was to liberate Hitler from his Munich surroundings, not to challenge his leadership of the movement. They wanted to impress upon Hitler the necessity for a programmatic approach on socialistic principles if the movement was to meet with success in working-class circles. When they called the Hanover meeting to adopt the draft program, they appeared to be sincerely convinced that they were acting in good faith and in the best interests of the movement. They believed that their draft program incorporated the true principles of National Socialism, which had been corrupted by the Munich clique composed of Streicher, Esser, Rosenberg, Amann, and others. They thought that Hitler had been misled by this group which had managed to isolate him from the outside world. The northerners wanted to reach Hitler and were confident that once Hitler learned of their position he also would accept it.

The most authentic evidence in support of these observations is Goebbels's diary for 1925 and 1926 (see also the documents in Jochmann, 1963, pp. 207–219). This diary, never intended for publication, was discovered in its original form after the Second World War. The entries represent Goebbels's feelings and attitudes in those years and provide interesting insights into party affairs.

On August 21, 1925, Goebbels noted that "Hitler is surrounded by the wrong people." Goebbels went on to state that the organization which Strasser and he were working on in the north would provide a weapon against the stale bureaucrats in Munich (Heiber, n.d., pp. 21–22). On September 11 he noted that Hitler appeared to be between the two camps (the north believed that socialism had to be achieved first to provide a broad basis for nationalism, and the south believed that the worker had to be won over to the national Idea directly), but that in principle he had already decided for the north (Heiber, n.d., p. 27). The continuing problem was Hitler's inaccessibility. "We have to get to Hitler," Goebbels wrote on October 19 (Heiber, n.d., p. 35); and again, "perhaps it will be possible to have a longer discussion with Hitler," he noted on November 2 (p. 39).

Goebbels looked forward to the Bamberg meeting with great hopes and expectations. He thought that Feder would be defeated and Hitler would adopt their point of view.[49] Then came the blow; Hitler turned against them. "I feel as if someone had knocked me on the head." Goebbels wrote after the conference. ". . . My heart aches so much . . . A sad journey home . . . I hardly say a word. A horrible night! Surely one of the greatest disappointments of my life. I do not believe Hitler without reservations any more. That is what is terrible: I have been deprived of my inner self. I am only half." (Heiber, n.d., p. 60.)

Goebbels idolized Hitler from the beginning and to find himself in opposition to his leader was an unbearable burden for him.[50] Hardly a week after the Bamberg meeting he wrote to Hitler protesting against Streicher's attacks upon him (Heiber, n.d., p. 61). He spent the next weeks in anxious waiting for Hitler's answer. On March 29 (Heiber, n.d., p. 68) it finally arrived; Hitler invited him to speak in Munich. Goebbels spoke in Munich, and at the end of the speech he was embraced by Hitler. "I am happy," he noted (Heiber, n.d., p. 71).

Goebbels was one of the leaders of the northern group in 1925–1926. He was the principal collaborator of Gregor Strasser and the coauthor of the draft program submitted at the Hanover conference. His recorded attitudes are certainly significant indications of the aims and purposes of the northerners in 1925–1926. There is no question that they never

[49] "Wir werden in Bamberg die spröde Schöne sein und Hitler auf unser Terrain locken." Heiber, n.d., p. 59; see also the entry for February 8, p. 58.

[50] Goebbels's adoration of Hitler is evident throughout his entries. See Heiber, n.d., pp. 27, 33–34, 39, 40, 43, 65, 71.

considered moving against Hitler, but hoped to the very end to gain his support.[51] Otto Strasser's biographer summed up the crisis correctly when he wrote: "They [the Strasser brothers] did not see the struggle in that light, they did not feel themselves to be working against Hitler. They only saw that Hitler was betraying the things he claimed to represent, the promise he had made, and sought to bring him back to them." (Reed, 1940, p. 80.)

The factional experience of 1925–1926 also demonstrates the pattern of Hitler's tactics. During 1925 he refused to take a stand in the dispute between the northern party leaders and the Munich office, to the great disappointment of Goebbels (Heiber, n.d., p. 27). However, the tactic of neutrality strengthened Hitler's position. As the issues sharpened, Hitler's arbitration became increasingly more important for both sides. Consequently both had to depend on his mercy.

Although Hitler was informed in November, 1925, of the intention of the northern leaders to form an association at the Hanover meeting in January of the next year, he did not voice any displeasure. (He was also informed about the National Socialist Letters, which were published with his knowledge and agreement (Jochmann, 1963, pp. 218–219).) He could easily have prevented the meeting at that time, but he remained silent. He allowed the meeting because he did not consider the programmatic arguments of Goebbels and Strasser threats to his authority. When, however, the second Hanover conference passed resolutions contradicting his policy on expropriation, he immediately convened the Bamberg conference.

When he finally made his move at Bamberg, there was no question of a party split. His decision was accepted by the north without a single northern leader's resignation. Under the circumstances there was no need to punish any member of the Association. He promoted the leader of the Association, Gregor Strasser, and a few months later appointed Goebbels as district leader of Berlin-Brandenburg. Participation in the Association did not affect the careers of such prominent functionaries as Erich Koch, Karl Kaufmann, Bernhard Rust, Victor Lutze, and many other lesser figures. The actions of the charismatic leader were not those of a victor but of a benevolent and forgiving arbiter.

[51] That they had no intention of deposing Hitler was illustrated vividly by their continued use of "Heil Hitler" in the 1925–1926 period (Görlitz & Quint, 1952, p. 256).

THE KAMPFVERLAG

At Bamberg Hitler did not voice any objection to that part of the Hanover resolution envisaging the Kampfverlag. The existence of a propaganda agency did not seem to contradict the principle of a totalitarian organization based on absolute leadership and a heterogeneous set of appeals; rather, it appeared a promising means to propagate the idea of National Socialism among the workers of North Germany. In 1926 Hitler's main concern was political survival, and although a separate propaganda agency under the direction of the Strasser brothers could not have been entirely to his taste, he could not afford to push his Bamberg victory too far. His control over the party was precarious;[52] the leadership he managed to assert at the Bamberg conference did not yet rest on a secure organizational foundation. Nor could he base his authority on mass support with any degree of confidence. The political climate of 1925–1928 was unfavorable for the Nazis, and in 1926 the party consisted of a mere thirty thousand members.[53] Hitler himself was for long periods of time prohibited from public appearances, which isolated him to a considerable extent from the political life of the country.[54] Under these circumstances Hitler chose to placate the northern leaders by allowing them to establish a separate center from which their particular brand of National Socialism could be propagated.

The political orientation of the Kampfverlag publications followed the spirit of the Hanover resolutions of the northern leaders; it was anticapitalistic, strongly nationalistic, and, in terms of international politics, pro-Russian. It is important to note, however, that except for its international orientation, the Kampfverlag policies were not opposed to what Hitler was saying from 1925 to 1929. Up to the economic crisis of 1929, the predominant note in Nazi propaganda besides nationalism was anti-capitalism and socialism. At party rallies the demand for a socialistic Germany complemented the cry for national unity.[55] In 1925 Hitler

[52] "At the beginning of 1926," writes Konrad Heiden, "Hitler couldn't have felt certain that he would still have a party behind him at the end of the year. On paper the party numbered some thirty thousand members. But these members looked to his untrustworthy subordinates even more than to Hitler as their leader." (1935, p. 113.)

[53] The year-end membership figures of the party were the following: 1925, 27,117; 1926, 49,523; 1927, 72,590; 1928, 108,717; 1929, 176,426; 1930, 389,000; 1931, 806,294; 1932, 1,414,975 (Volz, 1934, p. 13; Schäfer, 1957, p. 17).

[54] Hitler was prohibited from speaking in public until May, 1927, in Bavaria, and until September, 1928, in Prussia.

[55] At the 1929 party rally, according to reports of the official Nazi yearbook,

declared war on capitalism, whether Jewish or Arian, and warned in a letter dated May 22, 1925, to a Nazi youth group that unless the party became a genuine workers' party "it would go to the devil" (Broszat, 1960, p. 51). And no one spoke in stronger socialistic terms in this period than Hitler's protégé, Goebbels, who attempted to conquer the proletarian districts of Berlin with his National Socialist message.[55]

The socialistic orientation of the party from 1925 to 1928 was reflected not only in its propaganda but also in its membership. Nazism, before 1923 basically a middle-class affair, became after 1925 a movement with a sizable proportion of members who were workers and members of the lower classes. In the north and west the movement was made up largely of workers.[57] Joseph Engel and Reinhold Muchow began organizing party cells in industries in Berlin and then in other cities. Talks about a Nazi trade union were prominent.[58]

This decidedly socialistic orientation was, for a variety of mutually reinforcing reasons, reversed by Hitler in 1929. By then Hitler had decided that the time had come for him to break into national politics as a major political figure. This decision was promoted by the more favorable political climate after the economic crisis of 1929. The rapid economic dislocations significantly disturbed the political equilibrium temporarily established in the middle 1920's and presented considerable opportunities for new political groupings. The political future for Hitler seemed to lie, however, in the rightist camp. There was little chance for Hitler to exploit the situation on the left, for that side was strengthened as a result of the economic crisis. Among the rightist groups, however, the

---

"200,000 Germans demonstrated for a free and socialistic Germany," *Nationalsozialistisches Jahrbuch*, 1930, p. 130.

[56] That initially there was no conflict between the Kampfverlag policies and the official party line (insofar as one may speak of an official party line in Nazism) can be illustrated by the fact that several Kampfverlag publications were advertised by Goebbels as Nazi literature. In November, 1926, he suggested the *Berliner Arbeiterzeitung*, *Der Nationale Sozialist*, and *Die Nationalsozialistische Briefe*—all Kampfverlag publications—as official Nazi reading material. Goebbels also remained editor of *Die Nationalsozialistische Briefe* until September, 1927. On Goebbels's activities in Berlin, see Reinhold Muchow's reports to the party headquarters from July, 1926 to March, 1927 (Stanford University, Microfilm Collection, Reel 5, Folder 133).

[57] At a typical Nazi meeting in the Rhineland in 1927, two thirds of the audience was normally Marxist. It was from their ranks that the party had to recruit new members. (Hans Hinkel Papers, Stanford University, Hoover Library Special Collection; see also Czech-Jochberg, 1933, pp. 168–170; Görlitz & Quint, 1952, pp. 271–272.)

[58] By the end of 1928, fifty industrial cells were formed (Schumann, 1958, pp. 34–35; Görlitz & Quint, pp. 265–266).

new circumstances had a disorganizing effect; their predicament was not lost on Hitler.

There were other reasons for the reversal of the leftist orientation. By 1929 Hitler was beginning to realize that he could not pierce the ranks of organized labor, that Nazism could never hope to win the allegiance of the organized workers in free competition with the Socialists and the Communists (Schumann, 1958, pp. 3, 28–29). Trade union loyalty and class mentality were too strongly ingrained in the majority of industrial workers to make them abandon their associations for the vague appeals of Nazism. Nazism might make inroads into the working class, but it could never hope to be a national political force if it identified itself with the workers (Heberle, 1945, p. 40; Stephan, 1931, p. 576).

Furthermore, Hitler willingly abandoned the socialistic orientation because it also relegated him to the background and enhanced the prestige of Gregor Strasser, who was strongly identified with that position. The leftist emphasis put the people around the Kampfverlag and the northern district leaders into the foreground, concomitantly creating an unfavorable impression about the Munich group with which Hitler was more or less identified. As long as his party organization and leadership were insufficiently established and his public appearances were restricted, Hitler had had to reconcile himself to such a situation. But with these problems largely out of the way, he was anxious to recapture the limelight and the effective direction of the movement. He and nobody else must be identified with the movement and with the Idea, and the road to this goal appeared now to lie to the right.

Finally, there were financial reasons for an alliance with rightist groups. By 1929 the members' dues of a reichsmark per month, collections, and subscriptions—the principal sources of party revenues up to then—did not cover the costs of a large party bureaucracy.[59] If the party organization were to be maintained and the bureaucrats' loyalties held, new sources of revenue had to be found. Obviously, these were not to be had in the leftist camp.

The reversal of Hitler's political orientation was complemented by the correspondingly changed attitude toward the Nazis of the industrialist and conservative groups. The economic crisis of 1929 made it necessary

[59] Bullock, 1959, p. 120. Rudolf Olden questions whether dues and subscriptions had ever been the principal sources of the party revenues. Yet he fails to identify any other sources of revenue for the years after 1925. (1936, pp. 109–110.)

for big business to look for a broader sociopolitical basis for furthering its interests (Schäfer, 1957, p. 14). As a result of the notice taken of the Nazis by the monied camp, and as a result also of the fair showing of Nazi candidates in the communal elections of 1929, the Nazi party, an object of sympathetic (or unsympathetic) laughter before 1929, began to be taken seriously (Bölcke, 1930, p. 364). Soon the Nazis were to be approached for support and cooperation by such influential conservative leaders as Alfred Hugenberg and by members of the highest nobility. New sources of revenue opened up; the party was rapidly losing whatever working-class character it may have had. At last Hitler was approaching the center of politics.

It may be noted that Hitler was never identified with the socialistic orientation to an extent which might have hindered a later rapprochement with the right. Although he let Strasser and Muchow organize industrial cells, he prohibited the formation of Nazi trade unions. The organization of the industrial cells (NSBO) in 1929 did not constitute a trade union but a propaganda agency.[60] During the period of leftist orientation, Hitler maintained his contacts with the rightist camp, especially with industry. True to his principles, he never let himself be identified with any orientation except that toward total power. His perspective allowed him to preserve his tactical flexibility without impairing his mass appeal. The people were drawn to Nazism not because of its social program or their class interests, but because it rejected the status quo that they despised, as illustrated by the fact that despite the reorientation of Nazi appeals toward the middle classes, the proportion of the worker element increased in the Nazi membership from 1930 to 1933. (See Table 3.)

Although Hitler's political reorientation did not seem to have any adverse effects on the mass following of the movement,[61] it did conflict with the Kampfverlag, whose leaders not only refused to follow Hitler's lead toward the right, but actually moved even further toward the left. Since its establishment in March, 1926, the Kampfverlag had been taken

[60] Schumann, 1958, pp. 33–35; Schäfer, 1957, p. 14. The initials NSBO stand for Nationalsozialistische Betriebszellenorganization, or the Organization of National Socialist Industrial Cells.

[61] Contrary to Lipset's contention that the Nazis received the support of the middle classes because they were anti-big-business (1960, p. 133), in 1929 the Nazis could move closer to big business without losing the support of the middle classes, who leaned on big business to escape proletarianization.

Table 3. The Social Composition of the NSDAP, 1930 and 1933

Occupational Group	1930	1933	Increase in 1933[a]
Workers	26.3%	32.5%	108.4
Employees	24.4	20.6	85.9
Independent businessmen	18.9	17.3	91.5
Officials	7.7	6.5	84.4
Farmers	13.2	12.5	94.7
Renters	1.9	1.6	84.3
Housewives	3.6	4.1	113.6
Students	1.0	1.2	120.0
Others	3.4	3.7	108.9

SOURCE: Wolfgang Schäfer, NSDAP: Entwicklung und Struktur der Staatspartei des dritten Reiches (Hanover & Frankfort on the Main: Norddeutsche, O. Goedel, 1957), p. 19. Used with permission of the publisher.

[a] With base of 100 for 1930.

over by a group of intellectuals who managed to make the publishing house a going concern.[62] Their success swelled their already well-developed feeling of intellectual superiority to Hitler and the Munich party leadership. This led to their defiant attitude from 1929 to 1930 and resulted in a split in the summer of 1930.

Ideologically, the Kampfverlag circle was identified with National Bolshevism, the twentieth-century variant of Revolutionary Conservatism, a late nineteenth-century movement of anti-liberal, anti-Marxist, and anti-internationalist orientations. Suffering from feeble political organization, Revolutionary Conservatism remained essentially a spiritual, literary movement, carried on by a generation of intellectuals who fed on Nietzsche (Baumont et al., 1955, p. 349; Mohler, 1950, pp. 8ff). In its revolutionary aspects it was elitist, representing the late nineteenth-century revolt of European intellectuals against the idea of democracy and the "vertical barbarian invasion" (Meisel, 1958, p. 11). It was an attempt of a self-appointed (or, as its adherents put it, "naturally selected") few to organize the many—an attempt to bring about the organization of society by the intellectuals (Heiden, 1944, p. 105). It aimed at an organic national community led by a naturally selected

[62] In 1926 the Kampfverlag started out with two weekly papers, the Berliner Arbeiterzeitung and Der Nationale Sozialist. By 1930 it had three dailies in Berlin alone, in addition to daily papers in Brandenburg and Saxony. Der Nationale Sozialist was published in seven editions for the various parts of Germany. Besides its newspapers the organization published periodicals and books. See Volz, 1934, p. 14; Schapke, 1932, p. 50; Miltenberg, 1931, p. 87; Reed, 1953, p. 73.

elite, and it searched for connections and organic ties to restore the natural bonds of society that were dissolved as a result of the false principles of the French Revolution (Mohler, 1950, pp. 18–19; Baumont *et al.*, 1955, p. 319; Arendt, 1958, p. 117; Stern, 1961, pp. xi–xxi).

Its conservatism was based on principle, not on an immediate situation. Also, its conservatism did not imply a negative attitude toward change, which enabled the movement to maintain the seemingly paradoxical positions of revolution and conservatism (on the different kinds of conservatisms, see Huntington, 1957). Its conservatism differed from the traditional kind associated with Edmund Burke not only in attitude toward change but also in rejection of the past. The Revolutionary Conservatives wanted to be free of the past and to build their new society, not on the traditional foundations of "throne and altar," but on the people. The new national community was to be an organic union between the masses and the privileged, despotic political elite in whom the masses were to find their mystical embodiment (Baumont *et al.*, 1955, pp. 319, 334). The relation between the masses and the elite was to be direct, unhindered by intermediary institutions and traditional forms of authority (Kolnai, 1938, pp. 110–111).

In a sense Revolutionary Conservatism was an adaptation of traditional conservatism to the conditions of modern society. In the absence of strong particularistic loyalties, traditional institutions weakened and became increasingly inadequate foundations for the rule of the few. A new means of integration was needed to combat the "revolt of the masses." The answer was found in the myth of the elite, a group which, by providing the masses with direct identification, was to turn the revolt of the masses into an act of mass submission to the few.

After the war, intellectuals of the Conservative Revolutionary heritage became fascinated by the ruthlessness and energy displayed by Bolshevism, and they began to move toward it. Möller van der Bruck, Ernst von Salomon, Ernst Jünger, and many others were awed by the revolutionary enthusiasm of the Communist-inspired masses and were attracted by the opportunities such fanaticism offered for an elite. They became progressively more convinced that the idea of the Conservative Revolution could not be realized unless it incorporated the idea of socialism. As a result the Conservative Revolutionaries of the postwar period became increasingly anti-capitalistic, anti-reactionary, and socialistic.

In the revolutionary camp of the left there were corresponding attempts in the postwar period to accept the rightist idea of the nation. Some members of the Communist party, such as Dr. Heinrich Lauffenberg, Karl Radek, and Fritz Wolffheim, accepted the idea of the national policies of the Spartacus League. It appeared to them that the idea of international Communism was utopian and that the idea of the nation had to be accepted if Communism were to be realized.

By the end of the 1920's the terms "Revolutionary Conservatives" and "National Bolshevists" ceased to denote two separate and distinct groups tending generally toward an alliance and an ideological synthesis. By 1930 the two could be identified as they congregated in improvised organizations, clubs, and discussion circles such as the *Tatkreis*, the *Juni Klub*, the Kampfverlag, and later the *Schwarze Front*.[63]

Like the nineteenth-century Revolutionary Conservatives, the National Bolshevists remained numerically insignificant, isolated from the masses, and split into many groups.[64] Their political insignificance was due not so much to the esoteric nature of their Weltanschauung as to the lack of leadership and organization. As intellectuals they had insufficient political flexibility and skill to compromise principles for the sake of unity. Ideologically they suffered from their eclectic position, which purported to aim toward a compromise between the extremes of nationalism and Communism.

The Idea of the National Bolshevists of the Kampfverlag is difficult to summarize because of its incoherencies and internal contradictions. The point of departure was an organic community based on "Blood, Race, and God."[65] The Idea rejected the principles of liberalism, individualism, materialism, democracy, Marxism, capitalism, and Roman Catholicism. It emphasized the völkisch idea, based on a "space and bread community," leadership, and the mystical belief in the fatherland. The destroyers of the German soul and of German existence, it was maintained, owed allegiance to New York, Paris, and Rome, representing

[63] Three articles may be cited as good summaries of these developments: Ascher & Lewy, 1956; Klemperer, 1951; Paetel, 1952. See also Mohler, 1950, pp. 60–63.

[64] On three separate occasions the attempt was made to transform the idea of National Bolshevism into an effective political force. In 1919 a fusion of Free Corps units with revolutionary worker organizations was proposed by Wolffheim; in 1923 Karl Radek called for a common Nazi-Communist front in his "Schlageter oration"; and in 1930 Otto Strasser organized the Black Front. All three proved to be abortive.

[65] On the ideas of the Kampfverlag circle, see the writings of Otto Strasser, Richard Schapke, Weigand von Miltenberg (Herbert Blank).

capitalism, imperialism, and ultramontanism. The Weimar system was set up by these foreign powers to destroy the German volk: hence, it must be destroyed not by piecemeal reform, but by a total revolution. The army, the bureaucracy, and the economy were to be undermined by whatever means were available, including bombs, strikes, and assassinations. For the National Bolshevists everything was allowed; nothing tied them to bourgeois morality.

Their violent anti-Westernism and anti-capitalism led the National Bolshevists to advocate a strongly pro-Russian orientation. They regarded the West as the principal enemy of Germany and German culture; they feared the West and, owing to their feelings of cultural and racial superiority, regarded the East with benevolent paternalism. They envisaged a "League of Oppressed Nations," consisting of Germans, Russians, Indians, Arabs, Chinese, and other nationals rebelling against colonial rule. This giant anti-Western coalition was to destroy the barbarian principles of the French Revolution (see on this Miltenberg, 1931, p. 69, and Paetel, 1952, pp. 3, 234).

They sharply distinguished the movement of National Socialism from the party. They regarded the movement as rooted in the nineteenth century and in the principles of Georg Schönerer, Friedrich Naumann, and the youth movement. To them, the organization of the party in 1920 merely mobilized an already existing movement. Hitler's contribution and importance lay in his understanding and discovery of the basic principles of the movement that had made him its first great spokesman. The party, although it represented the movement, was never to be identified with it. It was only a temporary, imperfect political means, whereas the movement rested on eternal spiritual principles (Schapke, 1932, pp. 19–30).

It is not difficult to see how these ideas could conflict with Hitler's conceptions of his movement in general and his policies of 1929 in particular. It is also obvious that Hitler must have been aware of the inherent contradictions between the Kampfverlag and the rightist orientation of the Munich group as early as 1926. For it may be noted that the politically relevant ideas of the Kampfverlag circle—such as socialism, pro-Russian foreign policy, and revolutionary assumption of power—were all voiced at the Hanover conference. However, there are no programmatic deviations in an empty faith; the correctness of a program can be determined only in the particular situation. Until 1930 these ideas did not directly contradict Hitler's policies and hence did not produce concrete cases of conflict.[66]

By 1930 the situation had changed; in April, 1930, the trade unions in Saxony proclaimed a strike. They were supported by the local Kampfverlag paper, the *Sächsische Beobachter*. Hitler, pressured by the Industry Association, issued an order forbidding National Socialists to support the strike. Martin Mutschmann, the district leader in Saxony, a member of the Hanover group of 1926, and a man with strong working-class sympathies, obeyed Hitler and kept the party rank and file in line. The Kampfverlag paper, on the other hand, refused to reverse its position despite Hitler's order and continued to support the strike in direct violation of the party line (Strasser, 1948, pp. 99–100; Bullock, 1959, p. 140).

In May Hitler went to Berlin to confer with Otto Strasser.[67] He demanded the dissolution of the Kampfverlag and offered Otto the position of party propaganda leader in return. Hitler, obviously unconcerned with the programmatic differences between them, was not interested in discussing the issues of conflict but wanted an immediate and definite answer from Strasser. Strasser, on the other hand, insisted on a discussion of essentially ideological questions. He told Hitler that he would entertain his offer only after he had ascertained whether they were in basic agreement ideologically. Hitler, who was anxious to avoid a split just two months before the Reichstag elections, agreed, and a two-day meeting ensued between the two. At this meeting long-latent issues were brought out. Among these were absolute leadership and the role

[66] The advocacy of revolutionary methods by Kampfverlag publications was an exception in that they contradicted Hitler's policies. The circular of June 27, 1928, issued by Hitler reprimanded the papers for their revolutionary spirit: "Some papers have published poems and other materials which contradict Hitler's policy of legal action; they imply that one day the party will reach its goals by illegal means . . . But the 1923 type of action is over forever" (National Archives, *German Documents*, Reel 45).

[67] Of the original triumvirate (Gregor and Otto Strasser and Hans Hinkel), only Otto remained identified with the Kampfverlag by the summer of 1930. Gregor was devoting full time to his party organizational activities and had lost control of Kampfverlag policies some years before. Hinkel followed Hitler's turn to the right. In the spring of 1929 he justified the alliance with the right on the grounds that "every true German Socialist must form a united front" against the Young Plan. A few days after the Hitler-Strasser meeting, he wrote an article in the *Völkischer Beobachter* entitled "We Do Our Duty" (Hans Hinkel Papers, Stanford University, Hoover Library Special Collection).

of the leader, the socialist issue, the revolutionary versus the legal way to power, and foreign policy orientation.[68]

On the question of leadership, Strasser challenged Hitler's contention that the Idea and the leader were by definition identical. He argued that a divergence between the two was conceivable and that in such instances the Idea was to be regarded as decisive. This, of course, was inadmissible from Hitler's point of view, since it viewed the party in ideological terms—contradicting charismatic legitimacy and the principle of absolute leadership. Hitler told Strasser that the Idea and the leader must for practical purposes be identical; to assume otherwise would be "to accord the right to each party comrade to decide about the Idea, even to decide whether the leader is loyal to the so-called Idea or not" (Strasser, *Ministersessel*, pp. 8–9). This would involve the leader in constant disputes and would nullify the principle of leadership.

On the socialist question Hitler declared himself to be a socialist who had real compassion for the individual worker, but who refused to subscribe to any dogmatic definition of the Idea. For him socialism did not necessarily imply the nationalization of private property or the distribution of wealth—these socialist tenets should be considered tactical weapons to be used only when necessary. He declared that he saw no need to change the existing system of economic organization so long as it served the national interest. He also disagreed with Strasser's goal of autarchy and emphasized Germany's dependence on world trade.

Hitler disagreed with two other ideological tenets of the Kampfverlag circle. In foreign policy he rejected the idea of a League of Oppressed Peoples and spoke out for an alliance with England and Italy.[69] In the domestic sphere he rejected Strasser's revolutionary ideas and defended the principle of legality.

Their meetings ended inconclusively: their differences were exposed but no concessions were made, which demonstrated Hitler's point about the futility of programmatic discussions. Strasser refused Hitler's offer of the post of party propaganda chief, and with this their relation seemed to be at the breaking point. Yet, the expected break did not take place

[68] They met on May 21 and 22. The source for the substance of their discussions is Strasser, *Ministersessel*, pp. 10ff. See also Hans Hinkel Papers, Stanford University, Hoover Library Special Collection.

[69] Hitler had set forth his ideas on foreign policy only a few years before in his unpublished "second book," *Hitlers Zweites Buch: Ein Dokument aus dem Jahr 1928* (1961).

immediately. Despite Strasser's declaration that Hitler's position "made it impossible for Socialists to remain in the party" neither he nor his associates in the Kampfverlag offered their resignations. In his book Strasser gives two reasons for their reluctance to draw the necessary conclusions after May 22; both are significant for the nature of factional conflicts in the Nazi party. First of all, they did not leave the party "because there was still hope that Hitler had been impressed by the discussion" and might possibly leave the "Rosenberg line."[70] Second, they remained in the party because they did not want to jeopardize its chances in the provincial elections in Saxony to be held in September. Indeed, they cooperated in the election on Hitler's side.

Hitler similarly refrained from taking the strongest measures. However, he is reported to have ordered Goebbels to drive Otto Strasser's supporters from the party (Bullock, 1959, p. 142). In the following weeks associates of the Kampfverlag were excluded from party meetings on various pretexts, and Richard Schapke was expelled from the party by the party court (USCHLA) for supporting Otto Strasser's attack on Frick.[71] On July 1, Strasser addressed a telegram to the party leadership and handed it to Walter Buch, chairman of USCHLA:

In yesterday's General Meeting of the Berlin District Mr. Goebbels, after excluding me from the meeting, delivered an attack on me and announced that my exclusion from the party would follow within a week. To clear up the situation I requested a reply within twenty-four hours. Otherwise, I will regard my exclusion as accomplished. [Strasser, *Ministersessel*, p. 35.]

No answer was received and Otto Strasser left the National Socialist party. A few days later he announced the formation of the "Fighting Association of Revolutionary National Socialists."

The break was disappointing for Strasser, for only a handful of the faithful followed him. In fact, the split hardly left a mark on the National Socialist party, as the elections of September, 1930, were to demonstrate.[72] The small impact of the Strasser crisis of 1930 on the party

[70] Strasser, *Ministersessel*, pp. 30–31. Strasser considered Rosenberg his real enemy. Before his meetings with Hitler, he offered to go to Munich to discuss ideological questions with Rosenberg in a series of meetings lasting for about four weeks. This, of course, was rejected by Hitler.

[71] Strasser, *Ministersessel*, pp. 32–34. It is interesting to note that Schapke, not Otto Strasser, was made responsible.

[72] Paetel, 1952, pp. 13, 636; Miltenberg, 1931, p. 89. At the elections of 1930, the Nazi vote rose from the 810,000 of 1928 to 6,409,600.

membership has been ascribed to the defection of his brother Gregor.[73] It is not possible to tell what would have been the case had they maintained a united front, but it is unlikely that it would have made much difference. The resignation of Gregor in December, 1932, had similarly negligible effects on the party rank and file, as will be shown below. The crucial factor here, as in all other factional conflicts, was Hitler's authority and his image as the symbol of unity and the incarnation of the new order. Otto Strasser never had any popular support; what he may have had came from his association with National Socialism. There was no question whether he or Hitler represented National Socialism. The rank and file were unconcerned about programmatic details or orthodoxy; they were willing to leave those to Hitler. For them only the all-compassing Idea, personified in Hitler, promised a better and glorious future. The content of the new order was uninteresting so long as the idea was appealing.

The behavior of the participants in the Kampfverlag controversy followed the previous pattern of factionalism. From 1926 to 1930 it was not Hitler whom the Kampfverlag papers attacked, but Goebbels, Rosenberg, Pfeffer, and other "antisocialists." In the summer months of 1930 Otto Strasser was fighting to capture Hitler for his point of view. Strasser insisted on a discussion of certain basic questions of party policy because he thought he could convince Hitler of the errors of his policies; he attributed the errors to Rosenberg's influence. In this Otto acted very much as Goebbels had in 1925. Both he and Goebbels were convinced that Hitler was really on their side. This belief was so firm that even after the discussion between Strasser and Hitler had revealed that Hitler's position "left no room for a Socialist in the party," Otto still refused to leave the movement.

On the other hand, Hitler carefully preserved his neutrality in the Kampfverlag issue. He long refrained from intervention in the conflict between Goebbels and the Kampfverlag despite Goebbels's repeated requests.[74] His equivocal position from 1926 to 1930 was misinterpreted

[73] Gregor was present at the second meeting between Otto and Hitler, and he supported Hitler's position down the line (Strasser, *Ministersessel,* p. 17).

[74] The Kampfverlag attack on Goebbels started with the publication of the article "Consequence of Race Mixtures" in the No. 17 issue of *Der Nationale Sozialist,* which contained a scarcely veiled hint about Goebbels's clubfoot. Goebbels appealed to Hitler for protection, but Hitler delegated the problem to Hess. In the following weeks Hess was bombarded with letters from both Goebbels and Gregor Strasser (who was taking the Kampfverlag's side). Finally, Hitler intervened to end the

by Strasser just as it was by Goebbels in 1925. However, the tactic of neutrality reinforced his position as the ultimate judge in the conflict. Herbert Blank commented later that Hitler remained the arbiter to the end; "they leave him the last word" (Miltenberg, 1931, p. 21).

The Kampfverlag issue broke into an open conflict on a matter of concrete policy, namely, the attitude of the party toward the strike in Saxony. Hitler was as unconcerned with the programmatic difference in 1930 as he had been from 1925 to 1926, but he could not allow disagreements on concrete policies. When he did intervene, he was not the avenging leader intent on punishing those who disobeyed him. He went to Berlin not to expel Otto Strasser from the party, but to offer him a high position in the party hierarchy in return for closing down the Kampfverlag. When he refused to bend to Hitler's will, Strasser was forced out of the party, but those of the Kampfverlag circle who were willing to change their tune were not penalized in any way. Hinkel and Buchrucker, who were members of the Kampfverlag inner circle, were to hold responsible positions later in the Third Reich.

With the dissolution of the Kampfverlag, the history of the northern faction ends. From 1925 to 1930 the northern wing of the Nazi party could be distinguished by its quasi-independent organizational bases (i.e., the Working Association of the North and West and the Kampfverlag) and by its quasi-ideological orientation. The dissolution of the Kampfverlag deprived the north of a symbol and its intellectual instrument. The secession or expulsion of the Kampfverlag circle from the party deprived the northern wing of a group of personalities who had managed to preserve their intellectual and material independence of the central party leadership.

After 1930 there was hardly any mention of the "northern wing." From then on the north would be identified with individual personalities within the party but not with a common orientation. After 1930 the principal factional protagonist was the SA.

The resignation of Gregor Strasser from his offices in December, 1932, was only an epilogue to the history of the northern faction. The event had no programmatic significance and had even less effect on the party

dispute by publishing a statement in the *Völkischer Beobachter* of June 25, 1927, in which he denied the existence of any conflict between Goebbels and himself. This statement obviously did not touch the substance of the issue, but sufficed to indicate his support of Goebbels for those who chose to interpret it that way. See the pertinent documentation of this conflict in Heiber, n.d., pp. 120–138.

rank and file than did the dissolution of the Kampfverlag. Although Gregor Strasser did not represent any faction in 1932, his resignation and the events leading up to it are relevant to my subject because they illustrate his attitude toward Hitler. Strasser's actions in November and December, 1932, go far to explain his actions in 1926 and 1930, and they point to Hitler's unique position in the party, which was of greatest importance for the nature and outcome of its factional conflicts.

EPILOGUE: THE RESIGNATION OF GREGOR STRASSER

The crisis in the summer of 1930 was followed by a period in the history of the party when, aside from the SA crises of 1930 and 1931, intraparty differences were submerged in the common expectations of coming power. The unity created by the tremendous popular successes of the party between 1930 and the second half of 1932 was disturbed only by issues of tactics. Legality was paying off; power seemed within reach.

The victory of the July, 1932, elections raised high hopes in the party. Leaders and ordinary members alike assumed that the fight was over and that power would be handed to them presently.[75] The SA was ready to take over and "clean the streets" and "reckon with their enemies" (Heiden, 1944, p. 478). The smell of revolutionary change was in the air. Hitler thought himself near his goal. On August 5, 1932, he saw Schleicher and received what he thought was a promise of the chancellorship.

These sanguine expectations and the intraparty harmony were rapidly dissipated after August 5. It appeared that the election victory of July would remain barren of political results. Despite the impressive victory at the polls, power remained out of reach, and many Nazis started to worry about the future. Another time of troubles seemed to be approaching, and the prospect called for some radical reassessments of political tactics. It was a question of tactics, not a fundamental question, that precipitated the resignation of Gregor Strasser (Bracher *et al.*, 1960, p. 381).

[75] Goebbels, 1937, August 8, 1932, p. 140; "We plan to end this year by victory," wrote Hitler in the *Völkischer Beobachter,* January 1/2, 1932. See also Circular No. 31 to all local party organizations in Upper Franconia, December 31, 1930: "We stand just before the assumption of power" (National Archives, *German Documents,* Reel 19).

103

The apparent reversal of Nazi fortunes after August 5 was due to Hindenburg's adamant opposition to Hitler's becoming chancellor. On August 13 Hindenburg rejected Hitler's bid for the chancellorship on the grounds that the National Socialists did not have the requisite Parliamentary majority to sustain him. He offered Hitler the vice-chancellorship, which the latter rejected in accordance with his policy of "total State power or opposition" (*Schulthess'*, 1934, p. 140).

The impasse dealt a shattering blow to the hopes in the party only a few days before. Hitler considered the events of August 13 a personal defeat (Vogelsang, 1958, p. 86), and Goebbels noted a "strong feeling of hopelessness" in the party as a whole (1937, August 14, 1932, p. 146). These feelings were not unjustified, since there was almost no chance of getting a Nazi majority in the Reichstag in the foreseeable future. The policy of "all or nothing" seemed to have led to a dead end and begged for reassessment. The alternative policy of joining a coalition government was supported by such important party men as Gregor Strasser, Wilhelm Frick, Robert Ley, Franz Stöhr, and Konstantin Hierl (Olden, 1936, p. 267; Lüdecke, 1938, p. 392). They realized that the party could not afford to follow a policy of opposition for a prolonged period of time without endangering morale (Goebbels, 1937, August 12, 1932, p. 143; Lüdecke, 1938, pp. 348–349). The party had to move ahead if it was to keep its members' confidence and its image for the outside world. Many of the proponents of the coalition policy were in local Nazi organizations and were in close touch with the rank and file, which gave added weight to their position. Many of them were convinced that July, 1932, represented the apex of party fortunes and that subsequent elections would show a decrease in Nazi votes.[76] Their arguments, however, were rejected by Hitler, who stubbornly adhered to his all-or-nothing policy. He calculated that by withholding his cooperation he would force Hindenburg and Papen sooner or later to accept his demands (ironically, this was exactly Papen's calculation, in reverse). Accordingly, on September 12 the Nazis brought about the dissolution of the Reichstag, and the party faced its third major electoral contest of the year.

[76] In September Gregor Strasser prophesied a drop in Nazi parliamentary representation from 230 to 180 after the November elections (Woodward & Butler, 2nd series, Vol. IV, No. 27 (September, 1932), pp. 56–58). The prospect of another election was a terrifying one for the party (Goebbels, 1937, September 19 and October 15, 1932, pp. 166, 181).

The results of the November elections proved the pessimists right. The party lost two million votes—a fact of deep significance for an extremist movement based on the promise of proximate success. The odds against Hitler's chancellorship lengthened, and the issue of tactics—temporarily submerged for the duration of the campaign—rose again. This time, however, the intraparty disagreements over tactics were complicated by an outside factor in the person of General Kurt von Schleicher.

Ever since the fall of 1930, Schleicher had taken the view that the Nazis had to be brought into the government.[77] He feared that continued exclusion from power would result in the radicalization of the Nazis, that is, their return to revolutionary means. When in the course of his conversations with Hitler following the July, 1932, elections he realized Hitler's single-minded obsession with the chancellorship, he abandoned his earlier position and urged Hindenburg to accede to Hitler's demand.[78] He did this not out of admiration for Hitler or ideological sympathies with National Socialism, but because it seemed to be the only way to bring the Nazis into the government. The close connection between Hitler and Schleicher was revealed when Albert Krebs was expelled from the party and relieved as editor of the *Hamburger Tageblatt* because of his attack on Schleicher (Jochmann, 1963, pp. 387–389, especially Krebs's letter to Gregor Strasser of May 25, 1932). Soon, however, Schleicher had to reverse himself again when he realized that Hindenburg was unalterably opposed to Hitler's chancellorship. After August 13 Schleicher ceased to support Hitler's bid and adopted a new course that contributed directly to the split between Hitler and Gregor Strasser.[79] His new course was supposed to lead to the Nazis' association with the government in a "block of national-minded groups" led by Gregor Strasser. Schleicher was aware of Strasser's predisposition toward a compromise policy, and he wanted to utilize Strasser's position

[77] The following exposition of Schleicher's politics is based on his letter to the *Vossische Zeitung* (January 30, 1934) and Thilo Vogelsang's analysis (1958, pp. 86–118).

[78] At their meeting of August 5, Schleicher assured Hitler of his support. As a result, Hitler thought he was near his goal. See Papen's statement on this in Sündermann, 1964, p. 171.

[79] This is what caused the great consternation in the Nazi camp after August 5. Hitler was told by Strasser on August 9 of Schleicher's change of mind. Two days later Hitler went to Berlin to inform himself personally of the situation, and on August 13 he had a brief and undecisive audience with Hindenburg. (Heiden, 1944, pp. 479–480.)

and influence in the party for his own purposes. There was one further point of agreement between the two men which facilitated their rapprochement; Schleicher had manifested strong sympathies with the working classes, talked about socialistic reforms, and strongly condemned the reactionary policies of Papen's "baron's government." This earned him some respect in trade union and socialist quarters and made a Nazi-Schleicher coalition not at all repulsive for Strasser.

What actually took place between November 23, when the first Schleicher-Strasser meeting is noted,[80] and December 8, when Strasser resigned from his party offices, is still a matter of conjecture. According to Otto Strasser,[81] Schleicher offered Strasser the vice-chancellorship in November. Strasser communicated this offer to Hitler, who allegedly agreed to the plan—only to change his mind a few days later at the instigation of Göring and Goebbels.[82] Returning to Berlin, Hitler accused Strasser of disloyalty and deceit, whereupon the latter resigned from his party offices.

Otto Strasser's account is based on the mistaken supposition that Schleicher's prime objective was to induce Gregor Strasser to accept a place in Schleicher's cabinet. It can be shown, however, that Schleicher's real objective was to induce Hitler to accept a cabinet post and that he was merely using Gregor Strasser for this end. It was only after the abortive meeting between Hitler and Colonel Ott on December 1, when Schleicher saw the hopelessness of capturing Hitler, that he decided to offer Strasser the vice-chancellorship.[83]

All along, however, Schleicher was playing a double game. Although his essential objective remained Hitler, he did not mind creating the impression that he might come to a separate agreement with Strasser.[84]

[80] Goebbels, 1937, p. 209. The negotiations with Schleicher were a direct consequence of Hindenburg's second rejection of Hitler's bid on November 21 (Forsthoff, 1938, pp. 194–195).

[81] Otto Strasser claims that his version is based on Gregor Strasser's account of the events as related to Otto at their last meeting on May 9, 1933 (1938 and *Juni 30*).

[82] Hitler allegedly changed his mind when he was informed by Papen (via Göring and Goebbels) that Hindenburg was not unalterably opposed to his chancellorship.

[83] Vogelsang, 1958, p. 105. On December 1 Schleicher made a last effort to elicit Hitler's cooperation. He sent Colonel Ott to see Hitler in Weimar. By that time, however, Papen had talked with Hitler of a coalition government, with Hitler as chancellor. This was a much more attractive proposition, and Hitler decided to accept it. (Gebhardt, 1960, p. 177.)

[84] The Schleicher-Strasser conversations certainly aroused Goebbels's suspicions, as his diary entry of December 5, 1932, shows (1937, p. 216).

The possibility that Strasser might consider entering Schleicher's cabinet on his own was a frightening one for Hitler and an eventuality that was kept constantly before him by Göring and Goebbels. Schleicher played his double game in part to force Hitler's hand by threatening him with a party split, but also it gave him an alternative. If he were to fail with Hitler, he could still go through with his implied threat and make a separate deal with Strasser. This is what Schleicher was forced to do after December 1, when it became clear to him that Hitler had decided not to accept his proposition.

The victim of this double play was Gregor Strasser, who never realized to what extent he was being used by Schleicher. All through these weeks in November he was negotiating with Schleicher in good faith on Hitler's behalf (Strasser, 1948, p. 37; Meissner, 1950, p. 252). He sympathized with Schleicher's plan because he was convinced that Hitler's demand for absolute power would never be granted, and he was anxious to exploit the opportunity offered by Schleicher before the Nazis' bargaining position further deteriorated (Frank, 1953, p. 108). Strasser carried on the negotiations with Schleicher and played the messenger between Schleicher and Hitler while Hitler vacillated and played for time. Hitler's procrastinations confused Strasser, who had to continue his negotiations with Schleicher without definite instructions. As a result, he was constantly in doubt whether this or that action constituted a betrayal of Hitler or contradicted his will (Strasser, 1948, p. 137).

There are no indications that a Hitler-Strasser conflict existed before the first days of December.[85] Although Hitler was strongly inclined to support Papen's course, which promised him both the chancellorship and badly needed funds from big industry, he did not repudiate Strasser's negotiations with Schleicher until after December 5.[86] It was be-

According to Sündermann (1964, pp. 163–165, 172), Schleicher worked for a split in the Nazi party. This, however, could hardly have been the goal of his policies, which were more constructive and ambitious in design.

[85] Dr. Planck, Schleicher's Secretary of State to the British Ambassador (Woodward & Butler, 2nd series, Vol. IV, pp. 386–387).

[86] On December 5 Hitler held a conference on the issue of the Schleicher cabinet. At this time Strasser reported his last conversation with Schleicher and Schleicher's offer of the vice-chancellorship. The issue was still open and Strasser was still dutifully reporting to Hitler. (Goebbels, 1937, p. 216.) Strasser may have met Schleicher on December 3 without Hitler's knowledge, but any further suggestions that they may have been conspiring against Hitler appear implausible in view of Goebbels's diary (Domarus, 1962, Vol. I, p. 164).

tween December 5 and 7 that Hitler disavowed the Strasser negotiations and accused Strasser of being disloyal and trying to split the party (Heiden, 1944, p. 504). On December 8 Strasser resigned from his party offices; the resignation was published in the party press the next day.[87]

Judging from the available data, there is nothing to substantiate the contention that Strasser was plotting against Hitler and wanted to split the party.[88] As late as December 5 he faithfully reported the conversations with Schleicher that he was conducting on Hitler's authorization. Hitler's attack on him on December 7 came as a surprise not only to him, but also to the whole party.[89] Had Strasser had the intention of splitting the party and engineering a revolt against Hitler's leadership, he certainly would not have resigned from his important party offices, from which—if, indeed, from anywhere—a split could have been engineered. However, he not only resigned immediately, he also disappeared on December 8. He went to Munich and left from there for an Italian vacation with his family (Orb, 1945, p. 240). His sudden departure—unknown to everyone—disappointed the expectations of all who might have been thinking of following him. As it happened, not a single leading figure followed Strasser, although he was the most important party member after Hitler. He disappeared without creating any crisis in party unity. No purges were necessary; Hitler did not need to fear any mass revolts.[90] The moment Hitler turned against him, Strasser was discredited in the party, just as his brother Otto had been in 1930 and Röhm was to be in 1934.[91]

Strasser was fighting against Goebbels, Göring, and Himmler, not

[87] On December 9 the NSDAP press made public the following news item: "With the consent of the Fuehrer, party comrade Gregor Strasser started a 3-weeks' sick-leave. All further rumors in this connection are without foundation." (*Schulthess'*, 1932, p. 220).

[88] "At noon the bomb: Strasser resigns his party positions," wrote Goebbels in his diary on December 8 (1937, pp. 218–219).

[89] According to Heiden, on December 8 Frick prevailed upon Hitler to bring Strasser back. "But Strasser had vanished. With a friend named Moritz he sat in a wine room drinking and cursing Hitler. He wanted to go to Italy and predicted that within a month Hitler would come back crawling to him." (Heiden, 1944, p. 505.) It is highly unlikely, however, that Hitler would have consented to make up with Strasser, whose socialistic speeches embarrassed Hitler's negotiations with Papen and Thyssen.

[90] On December 10 Hitler took over the leadership of the political organization of the party and appointed Robert Ley as his executive (*Schulthess'*, 1932, p. 220).

[91] "The workers do not stand behind Strasser; they stand behind Hitler and Ley" (Thyssen, 1941, p. 127).

Hitler. He told Hans Frank in November, 1932: "It seems to me that Hitler is completely in the hands of his Himmler and Himmlers" (Frank, 1953, p. 108). Strasser wanted to do in 1932 what Goebbels and Otto Strasser attempted before and Röhm was to try later—namely, capture Hitler for his ideas. When Hitler decided against his coalition policy, Strasser was bitter and disappointed, but unshaken in his loyalty to Hitler. He told Rosenberg: "As a Hitler-man I fought; as a Hitler-man I want to go to my grave."[92]

[92] Rosenberg, 1955, p. 273. Strasser refrained from any attacks on Hitler during 1933 and 1934. He did not join his brother's Black Front. Hitler similarly refused to vilify Strasser; soon after December 8, 1932, he instructed the party press to stop its attacks on Strasser. There were rumors during 1933–1934 that Strasser might enter Hitler's government, but they did not materialize. Strasser was killed during the purges of June–July, 1934, but whether Hitler had anything to do with his murder is highly problematical. According to Rosenberg (Seraphim, 1956, p. 36), Hitler not only did not give an order to kill Strasser, but initiated an investigation after the purge to bring Strasser's murderers to account. Just a few days before he was shot, Strasser received his Honor Medal No. 9 ("Ehrenzeichen") from the party.

VII

The SA Faction, 1926–1934

THE relation of the SA to the party remained undefined during the first period of its history. Hitler himself admitted later that before 1924 he had no clear plans for the paramilitary organizations in the party (1953, pp. 217–218). During 1924 he defined the nature of the party fairly well, but did not form a comparably sophisticated view of the armed formations. The principle of absolute subordination of the SA to the party leadership in political matters was too simple to work. This principle, which guided the SA-party relation after 1925, mistakenly assumed the limits and the nature of the "political" to be ascertainable. Once this became the subject of controversy, the principle of subordination became less a guide than a source of conflict. The other problem that was to sharpen the issue between the political and the armed formations in the movement was one that is inherent in any relation among institutions. The SA was to be a separate, politically subordinated organization. As a separate organization with special tasks it quickly developed an ethos of its own, necessary for *esprit de corps*. This ethos increased the effectiveness of the organization, but at the same time separated it from the political organization. Members were imbued with a consciousness distinct from that of the "politicians"; they considered themselves good National Socialists and loyal followers of Hitler, but they entered these relations as members of the SA. There was a paradox here: the growth and effectiveness of the SA varied inversely with its relation with the party. The more successful and viable the SA became, the greater its *esprit de corps* and the greater the psychological distance between it and the party organization. Consequently, the most successful and able of its leaders were the greatest potential threats to party unity, regardless of their own convictions and aspirations. The problem of the SA in the party was not primarily one of particular policies, but was inherent in the nature of the situation.[1]

The idea of the Frontbann as an above-party, autonomous military organization dedicated to a national purpose was obviously incompatible with the principle of political subordination; hence the break with Röhm came soon after Hitler's release from prison. Although Röhm was obviously inclined toward a compromise and worked hard to persuade Hitler to recognize the Frontbann as a special arm of the National Socialist movement, Hitler was determined to break completely with the Frontbann. The new party was to be built of individual members, not of closed groups. Party membership would be the prerequisite of any secondary association, such as membership in the SA.[2] The Frontbann had to be repudiated, and its members were required to sever all connections with it before they could be considered for admission into the party.[3]

The repudiation of the Frontbann, however, did not mean the establishment of a corresponding SA organization. For a year and a half after his break with Röhm, Hitler postponed, for several reasons, the establishment of a central SA leadership. In the first place, it was necessary to make a complete break with the Frontbann, and to have erected a new SA leadership immediately might have created the impression that the SA was but a continuation of the Frontbann under another name. Second, Hitler had to establish his authority over the party before

---

[1] Herman Mau comes to a similar conclusion but for a different reason. In his view, the conflict was inherent in the SA-party relation because of the different sociological origins of the SA men. (1953, p. 122.)

[2] "Fundamental Directives for the Re-establishment of the NSDAP," *Völkischer Beobachter*, February 26, 1925. Whether Hitler was acting only instinctively, fearing the existence of closed groups in the party, or whether he was conscious of the psychological implications of his directives, is impossible to say. Clearly, the requirement that candidates for membership divorce themselves from all other associations fits into the proposition that the prerequisite of total loyalty is a psychological *tabula rasa*.

[3] Several local Frontbann organizations requested admission to the party during 1925 and 1926, claiming that they were and always had been loyal Nazis. They were all told first to disband completely and then apply individually for admission. (Correspondence between North Frontbann and Bouhler, November 17, 1925, and June 25, 1926, National Archives, *German Documents*, Reel 24.)

On June 3, 1925, the *Völkischer Beobachter* officially reported Hitler's declaration that the NSDAP had nothing whatsoever to do with the Frontbann.

he could think of organizing a new SA. Third, the prerequisite of an SA was the existence of local party organizations closely tied to the party central leadership. Finally, Hitler may have procrastinated because he was afraid of a centralized SA leadership in the first year of the party.

At the same time the necessity for and the political value of a strong-arm section were quite obvious and were recognized by Hitler.[4] Consequently, during 1925 and the first nine months of 1926, local party leaders were encouraged by Munich to establish their own SA units although they were not told about the SA organization, uniforms, or rules, aside from two principles which the local leaders were to keep in mind: the local SA groups were to recruit only from local party members, and they were not to carry arms.[5] Under the circumstances, the first SA groups were the creation of local party leaders who frequently became SA leaders. The SA was hardly distinguishable from the political organization, had no separate existence, and was under the absolute and exclusive authority of local party leaders.

The national organization of the SA commenced with the appointment of Pfeffer von Salomon as supreme SA leader (Oberste SA Führer —OSAF) on October 1, 1926. With the establishment of the supreme SA command, local SA units were separated from local party organizations and were ordered into a new hierarchy[6]; this could not fail to produce friction and jealousy. The situation grew worse in the coming years as the SA throve and perfected its organization. But the newly organized SA could not, for some years to come, repudiate its local origins. For the remainder of the 1920's, the SA continued on the principle of leadership at the local level rather than in the military pattern of an impersonal hierarchy with interchangeable parts. The local SA leaders were not just commanders acting under orders and receiving the alle-

[4] The importance of the SA in protecting meetings was reflected in the exchange of letters between Otto Telschow, leader of the East Hanover district, and Goebbels. Goebbels refused to appear as speaker in Cuxhaven because there was no SA to provide protection. (Correspondence of October 23, November 25, and December 6, 1925, National Archives, *German Documents*, Reel 21.)

[5] Munich was besieged by letters from local party leaders asking for directions concerning the organization and rules that were to govern the new SA. Bouhler's standard reply was that, until the establishment of a central SA command, no uniform rules existed for the SA. (Bouhler to Goebbels, October 2, 1925; Bouhler to Vahlen (Pomerania), March 2, 1926; Bouhler to Lutze, August 8, 1925; National Archives, *German Documents*, Reels 22, 24, and 85, respectively.)

[6] Circular to the district leaders, October 1, 1926, National Archives, *German Documents*, Reel 85.

giance of their subordinates because of their status in the hierarchy; they were also charismatic leaders who attracted comrades on the basis of personal loyalties and who managed to establish strongly disciplined groups of fanatical fighters. Although this solved the problem of discipline on the local level—a serious problem for any nonmilitary organization without the institutional means of enforcing rules—it seriously impaired the authority of the central leadership over the local organizations.

The new SA differed from Röhm's idea of a military organization, exemplified in the Frontbann, in its lack of strong hierarchy and in its political orientation. Association with the regular army was eschewed by Hitler and the OSAF, and particular safeguards were instituted by the leadership to separate the SA from other military organizations. The SA was forbidden to carry arms; its motto was "fight without weapons." It had military exercises, but its training program emphasized physical fitness and sports such as boxing, wrestling, and jujitsu that could be utilized for strong-arm purposes. In order to guard against a relapse into militarism, the leadership stressed in all SA units the necessity of political schooling under the direction of local SA leaders.[7]

The emphasis on political education usually had the opposite of the intended effect. Instead of strengthening the national leadership of the SA at the expense of the local leaders, it frequently supplemented the position of the local SA leaders and increased their autonomy. Although the party leadership and the OSAF directed local leaders to introduce political training courses in their units, such directives contained little more than a vague reference to the esoteric Weltanschauung. Under the circumstances, the local SA leaders had to rely on their own cleverness to provide political indoctrination; this, in turn, made for sharp differences between localities. Depending on their own backgrounds and political convictions, local SA leaders would stress nationalistic, socialistic, anti-Semitic, racist, völkisch, or conservative ideas in their units. This advanced the cohesiveness of the local groups and the position of the local leader at the expense of the national organization (Bracher *et al.*, 1960, pp. 841–842).

[7] SA Order ("SABE") No. 1, November 1, 1926: "The training of the SA has to proceed not according to military points of view but according to party considerations . . . The SA has to be ideologically educated, and thus should widen the horizon of every SA man." National Archives, *German Documents*, Reel 85.

Concurrently with these changes in the nature of the post-1926 SA, there were some noticeable changes in its leadership. As a result of the economic upswing and the withdrawal of support from the army, the fortunes of the numerous semimilitary organizations declined after 1925 (Bullock, 1959, p. 125; Bracher *et al.*, 1960, p. 847). Although the rank and file was gradually absorbed into civilian life, the leaders of these semimilitary organizations frequently continued their activities within the newly formed SA. These former Free Corps leaders severely condemned the policy of rallying behind the state, a policy adopted by the army under the leadership of General von Seeckt; consequently, they did not greatly disapprove of Hitler's policy of demilitarization.

Besides the former Free Corps men, the SA leadership soon included many questionable elements from among the unemployed and the criminals, men who did not have the soldier's mentality of former military men. After 1926 the members of the SA were more often young men of the postwar generation—it has been estimated that by the end of the 1920's only about twenty to twenty-five per cent of the SA members were veterans and former Free Corps men (Görlitz & Quint, 1952, p. 279). Hence, the SA, which before 1926 was made up largely of former military men of middle-class backgrounds and authoritarian orientation, became after 1926 a motley group of the most diverse social backgrounds and political beliefs. It was an army of the alienated, the confused, the dissatisfied, the lost. The typical SA man was for radical change, but had no clear idea about what form that change ought to take. He was bitter about present conditions and everything associated with them. He was a mercenary of undetermined future; he was a potential totalitarian fanatic.[8]

Although until the upswing of the Nazis' fortunes in 1930 the problems inherent in the relation between the SA and the party leadership were obscured by the common problem of survival, they were nonetheless real. However, this relation was considerably easier to formulate than to carry out. The document establishing the SA distinguished between political and military affairs.[9] The osaf was subordinated to the

---

[8] This was more true before than after 1930, when the ranks of the SA were filled with people who were committed to the idea of the SA only to receive free meals. For a description of life in the SA see "Was ist ein SA-Heim?" *Vossische Zeitung*, August 30, 1931.

[9] sabe 2, November 2, 1926, and grusa 3, June 3, 1927, National Archives, *German Documents*, Reel 85. Some of the provisions may be cited here: "No. 3. The

party leadership in political matters, but the SA was to have autonomous powers in military and technical questions, thus giving it a quasi-autonomous existence. Conflicts rapidly ensued between local party leaders and the SA command about the limits of the political and technical spheres.[10] Local party leaders looked with a great deal of suspicion at the quasi-private bands of local SA leaders and feared the loss of authority. The local SA leaders, and especially the former Free Corps officers, regarded local party leaders as social and intellectual inferiors and referred to them contemptuously as the "politicians" (Oehme & Caro, 1930, p. 40). The SA claimed with some justification that it carried the main burden of the fight, but that it was treated by the party leaders as an instrument instead of as an equal partner.

Similarly, the relation between Hitler and the OSAF Franz Pfeffer von Salomon was one of friction. Pfeffer was a former Free Corps officer and, from 1924 to 1926, the leader of the Nazi party in Westphalia and in the Ruhr. From the beginning of his appointment as OSAF, he attempted to combine Hitler's conception of the SA with his experience of the Free Corps—clearly an impossible undertaking. He agreed that the SA should be a military arm of the Nazi party, but beyond this overall subordination, he insisted on the right to make decisions on policy. Since he received the cooperation of former Free Corps officers, whose technical knowledge was necessary for organization, Pfeffer slipped into the old heresy of Röhm: the concept of an autonomous military force.[11] As the SA grew stronger, the problem of "relapse into the military conception" became more acute. The economic and political crises of 1929 not only reoriented party policies, but also affected the relation of the SA and the party. Close liaisons with the army were built up by local SA

SA is a means to an end. The end is the victory of the Weltanschauung whose carrier is the NSDAP. The carrier of the Weltanschauung determines what is to happen. The political leadership of the NSDAP determines what the SA should do, how we can help the NSDAP to victory. It is our task to establish the SA, to develop it, and keep it efficient. . . . No. 4. The political leader gives the SA its tasks. The SA leader is responsible for the execution of these tasks and has sole command powers during their execution. . . . No. 5. The SA determines whether the task exceeds its ability. Differences of opinion have to be referred to the next higher level. . . ."

[10] See for example Arthur Dinter's letter to Pfeffer, April 6, 1927, National Archives, *German Documents*, Reel 85.

[11] On October 13, 1928, Pfeffer reportedly said in Cologne that the SA was the carrier of the German army of the future, and that as such it had to be built up as a state within a state (Oehme & Caro, 1930, p. 40; see also Heiden, 1944, pp. 296–297; Grebing, 1959, p. 61).

leaders in direct contradiction to Hitler's principle of political subordination (Bracher *et al.*, 1960, pp. 846–848).

These inherent stresses and strains between the SA and the party leadership were complicated by the rivalries between SA and party leaders; in addition, there was conflict among the SA leaders themselves. All of these were difficult to resolve because the ties between local SA leaders and their subordinates made these leaders largely independent of central SA authority. The disadvantage of basing the local SA groups on the personality of the leader was now revealed: any disciplining of an SA leader might result in the secession of his entire SA unit. The economic crisis introduced another source of disagreement between the SA and the political leadership, the issue of political tactics. Hitler's policy of legality was questioned more and more by a great number of SA leaders, and these leaders voiced the sentiments of their radical following, who were flocking to the SA to escape economic hardships (Bracher *et al.*, 1960, pp. 846–848).

By the summer of 1930 the disagreements assumed serious proportions. In August, Pfeffer, resenting Hitler's interference in what he considered his sphere of competence and also disagreeing with Hitler's policy of legality, tendered his resignation.[12] A few days later, and quite independent of this action, the Berlin SA revolted against the Berlin party leadership.

The first revolt of the Berlin SA was the culmination of a latent conflict between the SA and the political leaders of the district. The Berlin SA under the leadership of Walter Stennes presented the party leadership with seven demands which, if granted, would have given the SA considerable independent powers. The Berlin SA asked that a fixed proportion of party funds be earmarked for it, that the SA be removed from the political organization, and that the party district leader have no jurisdiction over individual SA men (Drage, 1958, p. 74). Stennes also objected to the rampant corruption and bureaucratization in the party,

[12] Pfeffer announced his resignation in an SA circular dated August 29, 1930. He stated that his request for a "visible and material participation" of the SA in the coming elections had been refused. Then he concluded with his appeal: "I ask, since the German Freedom movement has to win despite incorrect developments in certain fields, that anyone who may want to leave the party should do so unostentatiously and only after the elections." (National Archives, *German Documents*, Reel 85.) In his farewell to the SA, issued on this same day, Pfeffer stated that he did not receive the necessary moral and material support from party leaders.

and he wanted a strong anti-capitalist and anti-Catholic policy pursued (Jochmann, 1963, p. 340).

Although the details of the revolt are of little consequence here, the way the rebellion was handled is germane to the subject of factionalism.[13] Hitler, who for several weeks declined to enter the dispute, was forced to act when the SA took over party offices only two weeks before the national elections. He flew to Berlin to pacify the mutineers. There he did not call on Stennes, but went directly to the SA troopers in their favorite meeting places, and by "promising, beseeching, upbraiding," he halted the revolt (Lüdecke, 1938, p. 320). His success demonstrated his unimpaired authority and the abiding confidence in him of the SA rank and file, and proved that the revolt was directed not against him but against the "bureaucrats" in the party.[14] The phenomenon is closely reminiscent of other intraparty conflicts. The mutineers believed that Hitler was really on their side and that the objectionable practices had been perpetrated without his knowledge. Hence, they appealed to Hitler several times before their revolt, which would never have taken place had Hitler responded to their pleas. But Hitler procrastinated and refused to act until the situation came to a head.[15] When he did act, his previously unsympathetic behavior did not seem to affect his authority —his charisma remained unimpaired.

The revolt did not bring about any purge of the ranks of the Berlin SA or of its leadership. Hitler promised to remedy immediate grievances; he raised the SA allotment from local party funds and agreed that all arrested SA men were to be defended in the courts out of party

[13] On the revolt see "Wie es zur Stennes-Aktion kam!" Stanford University, Hoover Microfilm Collection, Reel 4, Folder 83; Miltenberg, 1931, p. 76; Drage, 1958, pp. 72–75; Bracher *et al.*, 1960, pp. 848–849.

[14] This was expressed in a memorandum by Schneidhuber (SA leader for South Germany) on September 19, 1930. The memo is a significant historical document on the relation of the SA and the party and on the attitude of the SA toward the party. In his memo Schneidhuber contrasted the SA with the party organization. Whereas the SA was disciplined and was devoted to Hitler only, the party was undisciplined, and was filled with inferior personalities who posed as little gods in their limited spheres. Although the SA carried ninety per cent of the party work, it remained the stepchild of the movement and had become a stranger to Hitler, who surrounded himself with and was misled by unworthy underlings. It was not the SA which needed reform; on the contrary, the party needed a hierarchical organization and strong discipline on the model of the SA. (National Archives, *German Documents*, Reel 85.)

[15] Stanford University, Hoover Microfilm Collection, Reel 4, Folder 83.

funds.[16] The most important consequence of the revolt was Hitler's assumption of the position of supreme SA leader and his subsequent recall of Röhm as his chief of staff.[17] From that time on all SA leaders had to swear unconditional loyalty to Hitler, a policy repeated in 1934 with respect to the army. The assumption of the position of OSAF by Hitler destroyed formally—although not practically, as the history of the SA from 1930 to 1934 illustrates—the independence of the SA in military and technical matters. The political and the military commands were unified in Hitler, who assumed the power of appointment of the SA leaders and became the ultimate depository of all authority.

Röhm's return as chief of staff did not mean that Hitler had changed his ideas about the nature and role of the SA. He was recalled because Hitler believed him to be the only man who could infuse discipline and who could make the SA accept the subordination of the OSAF to party leadership.[18] However, Röhm's basic ideas about the SA had not changed since 1925, although he realized that he had to compromise them at least for the time being. He still thought of an above-party organization of combat leagues dedicated to an authoritarian state and based on military principles. From the point of view of the party leadership, his recall was but a temporary solution to the immediate problem of the SA.

As Hitler was to admit later, he had not in this period succeeded in finding an appropriate leader for the SA (1953, p. 374); the fundamental reason for his failure was inherent in the problem. To the extent that he wanted to see a powerful SA that could be used for political purposes, he was invariably faced with the rise of strong SA leaders who often developed independent views. On the other hand, the dismissal of men with strong personalities often diminished the importance of the SA. What Hitler wanted was a strong SA without independent personalities but with independent purposes—a thing he was to achieve in the SS after 1934. However, the SS was a specially selected group and grew to

[16] Hitler's order of September 2, 1930, decreed: (1) A special SA levy of .20 reichsmark per capita. (2) Increase in membership initiation dues from one to two reichsmarks. One reichsmark was to go to the SA. (3) Fifty per cent of the funds earmarked for extraordinary cases (Kampfsatzspenden) was to be paid to the SA by the local organizations. (4) Legal counsel was to be provided to arrested SA men and the costs to be paid by the local party organization. (National Archives, *German Documents*, Reel 85.)

[17] Directive of September 2, 1930, National Archives, *German Documents*, Reel 85.

[18] Röhm's first concern was to re-establish discipline and order in the SA. See his order of July 31, 1931, National Archives, *German Documents*, Reel 85.

power under an established totalitarian regime. The SA was a motley crew with diverse purposes and motivations and took shape in a society that offered several alternatives. In 1930 Hitler called Röhm back because he needed a strong SA. In 1934 he turned against Röhm and for practical purposes destroyed the SA.

The doctrine of legality and the rapprochement with the right appear to have been tactically correct, judging by the election victory of September, 1930. The weakening of nationalist and bourgeois parties indicated a fertile source of potential Nazi adherents at a time when financial assistance from business and industrial interests was becoming indispensable to the growing movement. Hitler's problem was keeping the legality without giving up the revolutionary image that provided the Nazis' principal attraction. Besides its psychological appeal for the masses, the revolutionary image effectively blackmailed the political and military leaders of the Weimar Republic. Hitler's solution to the dilemma was to emphasize that the revolutionary goals of the party would be implemented once state power had been acquired by nonrevolutionary means.[19] Quite paradoxically, this seemed to bother his allies on the traditional right less than it did the activist, radical segments of his party. The former, who should have been frightened away by such pronouncements, were not apprehensive, possibly because they interpreted them as propaganda designed for intraparty consumption. The latter, presumably for the same reason, grew increasingly uneasy about Hitler's tactics, which they saw as corrupting the revolutionary goals. Both believed that Hitler's revolutionary goals were propagandistic and that he could be won over to the principles of traditional authoritarianism.

Undoubtedly, Hitler's actions during this period provided legitimate grounds for the fears of radicals within the party. His assurances at the Scheringer trial in February, 1930, that the SA was not an anti-state force impressed the army but not the radicals in the SA. His increasingly close association with big industrial interests and traditional rightist forces deceived these people, but disquieted the radicals. It was mainly these tactics that made discipline in the radical-minded SA difficult to maintain and required the recall of Röhm.

Röhm took over the SA command on January 4, 1931, and immediate-

[19] This gave rise to serious problems after January, 1933, when the radicals in the party were pushing for a second revolution.

ly set out to reorganize the SA on lines closely resembling those of the army. Strong hierarchical organization centralized in the hands of the chief of staff of the SA (Röhm), who was in turn responsible to the OSAF (Hitler), was designed to destroy the independence of local and regional SA leaders. Specialized SA formations were organized, and a training college for SA leaders was set up in June, 1931. The membership drive (aided by the depression) raised the SA membership during 1931 from 100,000 to around 300,000 (Bullock, 1959, pp. 152–153). The relation with the army was improved when Schleicher decreed in January, 1931, that Nazi workers should no longer be dismissed from army arsenals because of their party affiliations, and when Röhm reciprocated by promising to dismiss all revolutionary elements from the SA. In February, Hitler issued a proclamation to the SA ordering its members to refrain from street fights and from carrying arms. In typical conciliatory fashion, he said: "I understand your distress and your rage, but you must not bear arms" (Heiden, 1944, p. 409).

These developments disquieted many SA leaders, who regarded such policies as dangerous to their quasi-independence. They were alarmed about the reorganization of the SA on centralistic lines, and they resented Röhm's purges of the SA leadership, particularly since the purged officers were often replaced by Röhm's homosexual friends.[20] The latent dissatisfactions erupted into open revolt in April, 1931, when Röhm purged the leadership of the Silesian SA and replaced the dismissed SA leaders with members of his intimate circle (Drage, 1958, p. 83).

Walter Stennes, representative of the supreme SA leader in the SA eastern district, appealed to Hitler against Röhm's action, but he was disregarded. A few days later Stennes was ordered to leave for Munich to assume a desk job at party headquarters. Within hours of Stennes's receipt of this order, every SA unit east of the Elbe telegraphed Hitler asking for cancellation of the order. In Berlin the party offices were

[20] Little is known about the sentiments in the SA vis-à-vis Röhm's policies. It appears that some resented his rapprochement with the army, whose discipline they dreaded, whereas others acceded in the hero worship and politicization of the SA introduced by Röhm. See Heiden, 1944, p. 409; Strasser, 1948, pp. 126–128; Görlitz & Quint, 1952, pp. 312–313; Drage, 1958, pp. 82–83.

Hitler defended Röhm in 1930 against morals charges by declaring that these were matters which should not concern the SA: "the SA is a collection of men for a particular political goal. It is not a moral institution for raising young girls, but an association of rough fighters." Private lives were relevant only when they contradicted the Nazi Weltanschauung. (Release No. 1, February 3, 1931, National Archives, German Documents, Reel 85.)

seized by SA units, as was the printing house of *Der Angriff*. Goebbels, whose fear of Röhm's growing power had led him to sympathize with the local SA leaders before Hitler's intervention, had to flee to Munich for the second time.[21] Stennes refused to obey Hitler's order and declined to meet with Hitler to discuss the situation.

With this refusal, the split was complete. Hitler wrote an article in the *Völkischer Beobachter* threatening with expulsion everyone who supported Stennes. A few days later he invoked the help of the Berlin police to force the SA to evacuate party premises. Then he went to Berlin to appeal personally to the SA rank and file and to "mobilize the street against the officers" (Görlitz & Quint, 1952, p. 312). Again he was successful. The SA followed him, and Stennes and a few other high-ranking SA leaders around him found themselves isolated. Their dismissal was effected without splitting the SA ranks, again illustrating that fact that there was no authority in the movement besides Hitler that commanded obedience and loyalty.[22]

After the revolt the centralization of the SA proceeded with increased vigor.[23] The leadership was purged and independent spirits were replaced by people loyal to Röhm. The hierarchical organization of the SA continued to be improved, and SA training was standardized on a national scale. These measures not only served purposes of the supreme leadership, but also enabled the organization to absorb the millions of unemployed who began to flock to its ranks.[24]

[21] The centralization of the SA command, to Goebbels's distaste, weakened the influence of local party leaders over their SA units. This explains his initial sympathy with the anti-Röhm faction in the SA. He reversed himself, however, when Hitler came out against Stennes. This has led some writers to observe that Goebbels played a double role in this revolt. See Bracher *et al.*, 1960, p. 852; Strasser, 1948, p. 126; Heiden, 1944, pp. 371–372.

[22] One of the several obscure aspects of the revolt is the relation of Stennes with Otto Strasser's organization, the Black Front. Some have maintained that Stennes was affiliated with the Black Front, but the allegation has yet to be documented. If Strasser was drawn into the conflict, his ineffectiveness would illustrate the limited appeal of his Black Front for the SA rank and file. (Heiden, 1944, pp. 371–372; Strasser, 1948, p. 126.)

[23] At the SA leaders conference of September 15–16, 1931, Röhm announced his reorganization plans, implying that many changes in personnel would be made. Then Hitler explained that Stennes left because he was not willing to accept the curtailment of his powers. Hitler recognized that the revolutionary fervor of the SA had to be satisfied, but not to the detriment of the party's policy of legality. (National Archives, *German Documents*, Reel 19.)

[24] By the end of 1932 the rise in unemployment caused SA ranks to swell to 500,000 men (Bracher *et al.*, 1960, p. 853). Considering that in September, 1931,

During 1932 the SA grew to be a formidable force within the state, and as such it aroused the concern of the army. Under the impetus of General Schleicher, the army command began to show interest in reaching some understanding with Röhm. Schleicher, who wanted to capture the SA for his own purposes, assumed a conciliatory attitude and became an important protector of the SA during 1932. Röhm, who wanted to bring all paramilitary organizations under his authority, needed the benevolence of the state authorities. The result was a tacit understanding between the two men. Despite suggestions to the contrary, there is no evidence that Röhm conspired with Schleicher against Hitler in 1931–1932.[25] He remained loyal to Hitler during the crisis of December, 1932, and kept the SA in line behind Hitler.

All speculation about possible collusion between Röhm and the army was set to rest after January, 1933, when the army assumed a firm stand against Röhm's plan to transform the SA into the National Socialist Revolutionary Army. This opposition defined the basic line of division during the crucial years 1933–1934. On the one hand, the army became the focal point of those who wanted to end the revolution by the liquidation of the Weimar system. On the other hand, Röhm and the SA formed the core of the revolutionary camp. Whereas after March, 1933, the army, conservatives, monarchists, and representatives of the upper classes wanted the re-establishment of order and the preservation of the status quo, those in the revolutionary camp, for one reason or another, regarded the achievements of January to March, 1933, as merely preliminary to the real revolution—some of these people wanted a second, socialist-egalitarian revolution to continue until it assured them of a prominent place in the government, and some talked about "permanent revolution." Thus, some wanted to see their particular ideas realized, others wanted economic rewards for themselves, and still others wanted further revolution because they were against any existing order.

It was paradoxical, then, that Röhm came to be the major figure behind the idea of the second revolution, for he had previously believed

the SA was estimated at 170,000 men, the increase for the year was remarkable. (National Archives, *German Documents*, Reel 85.)

[25] During 1931–1932 Röhm was Hitler's principal liaison with the army, which was represented by Schleicher. The Röhm-Schleicher conversations of 1931–1932 gave rise to speculation that, in return for Schleicher's benevolent attitude, Röhm pledged the SA to a national cause rather than to the political ambitions of Hitler. See Arendt, 1958, p. 318; Heiden, 1944, pp. 426, 450ff; Lüdecke, 1938, p. 332; Strasser, 1948, p. 136.

in traditional authoritarianism based on the military. During 1933–1934 he sided with the socialists, nihilists, and opportunists against such traditional authorities as the army, conservatism, and monarchism. But this is only one component of the complex movement for a second revolution, which was to culminate in the purges of June, 1934.

THE SA AND THE SECOND REVOLUTION

During the first months of 1933 the SA was the dominant instrument of the National Socialist revolution against the left. It was the symbol of Nazi radicalism and the principal guardian of the National Socialist Idea.[26] Its frequent lapses of discipline and its brutal excesses were dismissed as the inevitable results of revolutionary enthusiasm or condoned as the proper antidotes for the Jewish-Marxist-liberal conspiracy. Voices against its excesses were few and hardly audible from the national-minded groups, while the protests of the left wing were naturally disregarded.

Yet, for the overwhelming number of SA members, the achievements of the first few months remained inconclusive—except for a few of them, they were still the have-nots. Slowly it became clear that a radical reconstruction of society and the establishment of an "SA-Order" would entail a revolution not only against the left but also against the right. To stop the revolution with the destruction of the left would not materially change the situation; it would merely set up different rulers, whose attitude toward the SA would not be much different from that of their predecessors.[27]

By the end of March, 1933, the first voices for a second revolution

[26] Röhm's addresses and essays collected in the Hoover Library Special File convey his ideas on the role of the SA in the National Socialist state clearly and forcefully. See, for instance, his addresses to the Diplomatic Corps of December 7, 1933, and April 18, 1934, respectively entitled "Why SA?" and "The National Socialist Revolution and the SA." See also his essay "The SA: The Representative of National Socialist Germany."

Radical activism was one of the SA's officially stated attributes: "The SA man is the holy Freedom Fighter. The party member is the clever agitator. The political propagandist has to enlighten his opponent, has to dispute with him, has to understand his point of view. But when the SA appears all this stops. The SA knowns no concessions. It strikes out for everything. It knows only the motto: 'Strike them dead. It is either you or me.'" (SABE 3, November 3, 1926, National Archives, *German Documents*, Reel 85 (paraphrased).)

[27] According to Rudolf Diels, the Gestapo had to fight harder against the SA in 1933 than against the Communists (*Trial*, Doc. 2460-PS, Vol. XXX, pp. 547–549, and Document 2544-PS, Vol. XXX, pp. 600–602).

against the right were beginning to be heard. Although the term "second revolution" was first used in this sense by Röhm in April, 1933, its appeals were not restricted to the SA.[28] "Second revolution" came to stand for the deeply ingrained feelings in the party of anti-capitalism, anti-conservatism, and general radicalism. In the spring of 1933 this radical spirit took hold of the party and there were signs that a new revolution was already under way.[29]

The popularity of a second revolution was especially great among those whom the first revolution failed to benefit materially and socially. The majority of party members belonged to this group, but the most ardent believers in further radical changes were those for whom the party was not merely a part-time political activity, but their sole livelihood. To this most radically disposed group belonged the millions of the SA.

In the 1930's the SA had become a turbulent army of revolutionaries, difficult to control and dangerous to rely on. It attracted to its ranks the poor, the unemployed, the dissatisfied, the alienated.[30] The past experience of such people and their activistic predisposition made them the truly revolutionary arm of the party. The SA was born in battle, designed for battle, and felt superfluous without the prospect of battle (*Trial*, Doc. 2168-PS, Vol. XXIX, pp. 279–308).

It would be difficult to categorize the SA by traditional left-right distinctions. Its heterogeneous membership was reflected in the multiplicity of political strains that came to characterize the SA.[31] Basically, the

[28] Goebbels and Rosenberg were especially vocal for a second revolution. In the summer of 1933 both assured the people that all that had gone before was nothing and that the revolution was only beginning. (Woodward & Butler, 2nd series, No. 247 (July 11, 1933), pp. 409–414.)

[29] Not only the SA, but local party officials had started to expropriate business funds, to the delight of the radical rank and file. "This was the time of little Hitlers . . ." (Bracher *et al.*, 1960, p. 902; Heiden, 1944, p. 640).

[30] By this time the SA included many former members of the Communist party. That this did not disturb the Nazi leadership, which never cared about the previous political activities of its members, can be illustrated by an amusing incident. On September 16, 1933, Hess wrote to the OSAF asking whether there were any former Communists in the SA who would be willing to testify against van der Lubbe that the Reichstag fire was planned by the Communist party. (National Archives, *German Documents*, Reel 85. See also Diels's affidavit, *Trial*, Doc. 405, Vol. XXX, pp. 569–571; Lüdecke, 1938, p. 598.)

[31] The lack of ideological orientation in the SA was revealed at the leaders conference of September 15 and 16, 1931, when Colonel Hofmann stated in Hitler's presence that he did not subscribe to a National Socialist ideology (National Archives, *German Documents*, Reel 85).

political orientation of the SA was nihilistic. The typical SA man believed in a permanent revolution without concrete goals or limits. His chief concern was the next day; his chief fear was becoming superfluous. His total dependence on the movement infused him with a generous dose of opportunism because, as Rudolf Olden observed, he was obliged not only to live *for* his ideals, but *on* them.[32]

Whereas the millions in the SA[33] and the radical spirits in the party lined up behind the idea of a second revolution, the forces of the right, led by the military, pressed Hitler to curtail the radical wave and to stop further revolutionary attempts. Characteristically, Hitler vacillated, moved closer to one side and then to the other, and spoke the language of the radicals while going along with the moderates.[34] Until June, 1934, he masterfully preserved his central position as the ultimate arbiter whose favors both sides sought; up to the very end people were guessing which side he would endorse.[35] Hitler's behavior was not motivated by merely tactical considerations—he found himself in a real dilemma. Politically and emotionally he was in sympathy with the radicals, and his antipathy toward the members of the old upper classes was notorious. Yet, the arguments against further revolution began to impress

[32] Olden, 1936, p. 214. Hitler's characterizations of the SA in this period deserve mention for their perceptiveness. In a cabinet meeting on July 3, 1934, he described the SA as an organization composed of the most diverse groups, who agreed only on the necessity of change (cf. the minutes of the Conference of Ministers, July 3, No. 55, pp. 118–122). In his Reichstag speech of July 13, 1934, Hitler explained the events leading up to the purges. He spoke of "those revolutionaries whose former relations to the State were shattered by the events of 1918; they became uprooted and thereby lost altogether all sympathy with any ordered human society. They became revolutionaries who favored revolution established as a permanent condition."

Later in his speech he characterized such people even more precisely: "without realizing it they have found in nihilism their final confession of faith. Incapable of any true cooperation, with a desire to oppose all order, filled with hatred against all authority, their unrest and disquietude can find satisfaction only in some conspiratorial activity of the mind perpetually plotting the disintegration of whatever at any moment may exist." (Hitler's speech in the Reichstag, July 13, 1934, in Baynes, 1942, Vol. I, pp. 290–328.)

[33] By June, 1934, there were over four million men in the SA (*Trial*, Doc. SA 156, Vol. LXII, pp. 422–423).

[34] At the SA leaders conference (July 1–3, 1933), Hitler said that the revolution as a forceful act against outside enemies was closed, but that the real revolution was still ahead. The real revolution would mean the transformation of man and the total transformation of state and society. (Bracher *et al.*, 1960, p. 898.)

[35] To the very last Röhm refused to believe that Hitler was against him. He thought, like so many factional leaders before him, that Hitler was in the hands of stupid or dangerous people. (Rossbach, 1950, p. 151.)

him. He wanted to speed up economic recovery, but found himself dependent upon the cooperation of the industrial powers (Woodward & Butler, 2nd series, No. 247 (July 11, 1933), pp. 409–414). He was eager to preserve the confidence of the army and of Hindenburg and worried about the possibility of foreign intervention should there be extreme internal chaos. Finally, by midsummer, 1933, the specter of a rightist alliance against him began to haunt him.

Hitler's ambivalent attitude toward the radical wing in the movement resulted in an uneasy stalemate, broken suddenly by the purges of June, 1934. During the stalemate Hitler instituted measures that strongly implied that he had sided with the conservatives,[36] but at the same time he frequently paid lip service to the idea of further revolutionary changes.[37] This attitude enabled the radical wing to survive and deluded many of its adherents into believing that Hitler was really on their side, although he was forced to play a double game because of pressures from the right. As a consequence, Röhm, Goebbels, and other loyal Hitlerites continued to make speeches against the existing state of affairs, and these speeches were never directly disavowed by Hitler.[38] Despite Röhm's revolutionary speeches, there were no recorded Hitler-Röhm conversations during the fall and winter of 1933–1934 to indicate a split between the two men.

In the spring of 1934 the role of the SA in the state became an increasingly important issue for two important powers, one foreign and one domestic. The French began to press German leaders about the military nature of the SA, which they regarded as a violation of Germany's treaty commitments.[39] Hitler, who was anxious to avoid international

[36] In April, the SA was deprived of its police powers, and local party leaders were specifically forbidden to interfere with business concerns. In July, Hitler instructed the state governors to make appointments according to merit, not political considerations. In August, the special SA auxiliary police force was dismissed in Prussia. In May, the British ambassador reported that the revolutionary movement had ended. (See *Trial*, Doc. 2371-PS, Vol. XXX, pp. 287–289; and the following dispatches of the British ambassador in Woodward & Butler, 2nd series, Vol. VI, No. 130 (May 10, 1933), pp. 219–222; No. 247 (July 11, 1933), pp. 409–414; No. 332 (August 15, 1933), pp. 505–511; also, Heiden, 1944, pp. 724ff; Greenwood, 1934, p. 162.)

[37] In his New Year's message to Röhm, Hitler praised the past role of the SA and wrote: "the task of the SA is to secure the victory of the National Socialist revolution and the existence of the National Socialist state and the community of our people in the domestic sphere" (Baynes, 1942, Vol. I, p. 289).

[38] See Röhm's speeches of August 6 and November 5; see also Goebbels's speech of January 14, 1934, in *Schulthess'*, Vol. LXXV, pp. 14–15.

[39] See Woodward & Butler, 2nd series, Vol. VI, No. 120 (December 9, 1934), pp.

conflict while he was consolidating his power at home, assured France repeatedly that the SA was a nonmilitary organization, although this disquieted Röhm and satisfied neither the French nor the army.[40] The army was beginning to be gravely concerned about Röhm's activities. Early in February, Röhm sent a memorandum to the ministry of the army in which he claimed the whole field of national defense for the SA—the sole duty of the army was to train officers and men for the SA. In the same month Röhm issued an order establishing a machine-gun company in every SA group (*Trial*, Doc. 951D., Vol. XXXVI, pp. 72–74). In March, Röhm handed Hitler a detailed plan for the establishment of a *Volksheer*, or People's Army, in place of the *Reichswehr*. The plan provided for the fusion of the SA with the army, a possibility which had been consistently resisted by the army leadership.

The disquietude in army circles affected Hitler not only because of immediate power considerations and the fear of a civil war, but because it was related to the question of presidential succession. Hitler could not hope to succeed Hindenburg in the presidency without the support of the army; but clearly no such support would be forthcoming until Hitler had declared himself unequivocally against Röhm's plans. These reasons —fear of a French intervention, fear of an army *coup d'état*, and fear of losing the presidency—appeared compelling enough to Hitler in the spring of 1934 for him to decide against Röhm's plans and come to terms with the military.[41] With this step, the issue of the second revolution and the SA entered its final phase, to climax in the purges of June and July.

Before considering the events of June, it may be noted that this decision by no means implied that Hitler was willing to play the role Papen had intended for him originally. Although he realized the necessity to come to terms with the right, Hitler remained much concerned with the

179–180; No. 295 (February 18, 1934), pp. 433–434; No. 302 (February 21, 1934), pp. 448–449; No. 303 (February 21, 1934), pp. 450–451; No. 305 (February 22, 1934), p. 462; No. 338 (March 8, 1934), pp. 535–536.

[40] Hitler insisted that the SA was a nonmilitary organization because its members carried no arms, they received no instruction in the use of arms, they did not participate in military maneuvers, and they had no connections with the officers of the regular army. Perhaps the only one who believed these barefaced lies was the British ambassador. (Woodward & Butler, 2nd series, Vol. VI, No. 295 (February 18, 1934), pp. 433–434; No. 302 (February 21, 1934), pp. 448–449; No. 305 (February 22, 1934), p. 462.)

[41] The exact date of Hitler's conversion is a matter of conjecture. Bracher believes that Hitler made up his mind against Röhm in February; Bullock thinks it was in April (Bracher *et al.*, 1960, pp. 943–944; Bullock, 1959, p. 263).

domination of the state by forces of the traditional right, especially when he was being increasingly pressed toward them. While he was vacillating between the army and the SA, he could maintain his position by playing one against the other. By abandoning the SA he deprived himself of a strong means of negotiation with the right and courted the danger of becoming the tool of his new allies.[42] To avoid this at the moment when he decided to throw the SA to the rightist wolves, Hitler decided to give his attention to another means of power— in fact, to another kind of revolution (Bramstedt, 1945, p. 74).

The appointment of Himmler as chief of the Prussian secret police on April 20, 1934, accelerated this new kind of revolution, although it had been proceeding quietly during the previous year, when members of the SS were infiltrating the conservative camp. Himmler's appointment symbolized the continuation and strengthening of this second, silent revolution.[43]

During June, Hindenburg seemed to influence Hitler decisively. He saw Hitler twice, on May 28 and on June 21, and Hitler acted after each interview. The problem of succession was becoming acute, and Hitler was determined to win the presidency even if it meant the dissolution of the SA and another parting of the ways with Röhm.

On May 28, Hitler was received by Hindenburg and reportedly agreed to curtail the military activities of the SA. On May 29, von Neurath told the British ambassador that Hitler had already given orders that all military exercises of the SA should cease. The British ambassador reported to London that the president and the army were convinced that Germany would stand a much better chance of getting her 300,000-man army and her other defensive requirements approved by the French and the British if the SA were played down. "Hitler agreed with them," he went on, presumably reporting what he had been told by von Neurath, "and is sending the SA on leave." He further reported that Hitler

[42] According to the British ambassador, this was an important consideration in Hitler's mind (Woodward & Butler, 2nd series, Vol. VI, No. 433 (May 30, 1934), p. 715).

[43] Although Himmler was at heart a radical, he was the chief figure in the purges of 1934. His own convictions did not matter to him because he was a true totalitarian, and thus was loyal to the idea of loyalty. In 1943 he said: "On June 30, 1934, we did our duty when we were commanded to shoot our comrades who made a mistake; we all dreaded it but we did it and we knew we would do it again when ordered and when it was necessary" (speech in Poznan, October 4, 1943, *Trial*, Doc. 1919-PS, Vol. XXIX, pp. 110–173).

was considering simply not recalling the great body of the SA after their leave.[44]

On June 4, Hitler had a four- to five-hour conversation with Röhm. Although no record of their conversation is available, it seems that they agreed on the necessity of acting covertly for a while in order to dissipate tension and rightist concern. Neither Hitler nor anyone else suggested that their meeting was a stormy one. It is probable that Röhm left thinking that Hitler was on his side but under tremendous pressures that compelled him to ask for curtailment of SA activities. This contention is supported by Hitler's report to his cabinet on July 3 that, after their talk of June 4, Röhm assured the SA leaders that Hitler was being severe only because of the international situation and that Hitler himself really shared his views.[45] Hitler intimated in his report that this was a deliberate deception on Röhm's part and accused Röhm of going back on the promise he had given on June 4. But Hitler never spelled out the substance of this alleged promise, and on the basis of indirect evidence and subsequent events, it may be fair to assume that Röhm was not acting in bad faith, but sincerely believed that although exigency dictated Hitler's actions, there was no fundamental disagreement between them.

On June 8, Röhm's official declaration appeared in the press announcing that for reasons of health he would commence a month's leave of absence. In this declaration he included a special note of warning to all those who might interpret his leave of absence as signifying the end of the SA.

I have decided to take the advice of my doctors and to restore, by means of a cure, my physical powers . . . The year 1934 will claim the entire energy of all fighters of the SA. I therefore recommend all SA leaders to begin to arrange leave now in June. In particular, all SA leaders and men who must be available for duty in July should be granted leave in June. In this way the month of June will be a time of complete relaxation and recreation for a considerable part of the SA leaders and men, and the month of July for the mass of the SA. I expect that on the first of August the SA will be once more ready for duty, completely

---

[44] Woodward & Butler, 2nd series, No. 433 (May 30, 1934), p. 715. In view of things to come, the above report may well have reflected accurately the substance of the May 28 meeting.

[45] *Documents on German Foreign Policy,* Series C, Vol. III, Doc. 55, pp. 118–122. This may well have been the case. In his Reichstag speech of July 13, Hitler said: "I warned him about chaos, assured him that the SA will not be dissolved, implored him to stop this development. Röhm assured me that the reports were exaggerated and that he would set them right." (Baynes, 1942, Vol. I, pp. 290–328.)

rested and restored in order to fulfill the honorable and heavy duties which the people and the fatherland are entitled to expect from it. If the enemies of the SA like to indulge in the hope that the SA will not return from leave, or return only in part, we are ready to leave them to the enjoyment of this brief pleasure of expectation. They will receive an appropriate answer at the time and in the form which may appear suitable.

The declaration concluded: "The SA is, and will remain, the arbiter of Germany's Fate" (Woodward & Butler, 2nd series, No. 448 (June 9, 1934), pp. 742–743).

This pronouncement was not calculated to allay the fears of those who were concerned about the SA, and the problem continued to plague Hitler until the last days of June. Although he had already decided to side with the army against Röhm, Hitler was not sure what was to be done with the SA. The army wanted its dissolution, but dissolution was not in Hitler's mind; as a consequence, the situation remained unresolved.

The crisis flared up again on June 17, when Papen delivered his Marburg speech. The speech was a plea of the conservatives against totalitarianism in general and against the idea of the second revolution in particular. It was a declaration of warning which Papen hoped would force Hitler to his knees because he would know that the army and Hindenburg were behind it.[46] The speech was a bombshell, and for four days it was difficult to tell what Hitler's reaction would be. The first response of the Nazis was to close their ranks in common opposition to the reactionary right. On June 21, Goebbels made a violent speech against "critics and reactionaries," in which he said:

The people will not forget the time when governments by divine right ruled. When we came to power this clique was against us. Now they stand next to us and offer their criticism. They want to remember that intelligence is not to be found only among gentlemen in club chairs. The

[46] The effect of Mussolini's advice to Hitler on the latter's visit on June 14 and 15 may also have influenced Hitler's later actions against the SA. At this time Mussolini advised him to suppress the radical elements in his party for reasons of foreign policy. Mussolini is reported to have told him that revolutions are made by one set of men, but governed by another. Hitler's respect for Mussolini at this time was considerable, and it is likely that he valued his advice. Otto Strasser relates that Mussolini was advised by the German Ambassador von Hassell, who, in turn, was instructed by Papen and Neurath. Hitler was informed of this by Goebbels on his arrival in Munich, and hearing it flew into a rage against the reactionaries. He met with Röhm in Munich and promised him to take up the whole question with Hindenburg. (Strasser, 1938, pp. 87–88.)

National Socialist government would have done better to place all these fine gentlemen behind locks and bars. [New York *Times*, June 22, 1934.]

Rosenberg echoed these beliefs when he declared in the *Völkischer Beobachter* that the revolution was not made in order that an antiquated class should proclaim the restoration of conditions outmoded by five hundred years (New York *Times*, June 20, 1934). On June 18, Göring threatened with punishment everyone who had any ideas contrary to Hitler's will:

The application of new and perhaps still more radical revolutionary methods will scarcely produce an improvement. It is not up to us to determine whether a second revolution is necessary. The first revolution was ordered by the Führer and it has been ended by the Führer. If the Führer wishes a second revolution, then we will be on the streets tomorrow. If he does not wish it, then we will crush everybody who tries to make such a revolution against his will.[47]

Such sentiments were not lost on the SA, and there were rumors of pending SA revolts (New York *Times*, June 24, 1934). Hitler was reported to have resumed contact with Gregor Strasser and was keeping in touch with Röhm (Strasser, 1938, p. 93). Meanwhile, Hindenburg sent a telegram to Papen congratulating his "best comrade" on his speech. The industrialists similarly indicated their sympathy, and there was no question where the army stood (New York *Times*, June 20, 22, 1934). The January, 1933, alliance seemed to have come to an end, and the division between the former allies began to assume dangerous proportions. The crisis was climaxed not by a civil war, as many feared, but by another Hindenburg-Hitler conference.

The first announcement of the meeting of June 21 stated that Hitler was "summoned" by the President (New York *Times*, June 24, 1934). This was later retracted, and the initiator of the meeting was not revealed. Both men had reasons to seek the conference. According to Strasser, it was Hitler who wanted to see Hindenburg so that he might discuss with him the need to reshuffle the cabinet.[48] On the other hand, Hindenburg was anxious to avoid a clash with the Nazis, for it might

[47] Göring's speech before the Prussian State Council, *Schulthess'*, Vol. LXXV, p. 154.
[48] Otto Strasser relates how Hitler was received by Blomberg and Göring. They were in uniform, and made a deep impression on Hitler. He also mentions that Hindenburg threatened Hitler with a state of emergency. (Strasser, 1938, p. 93; *id*, 1948, p. 182.)

have resulted in a civil war. There are no minutes available of their conversations, but judging from the events to come, the conference had a decisive influence on Hitler. In the following days the violent attacks on the "reaction" ceased, and on June 24, Hitler is reported to have told the *News Chronicle* that even old friends might have to be disavowed for the sake of the movement (Strasser, *30 Juni*, p. 66). That an agreement was reached with the right is indicated by Papen's speech in the Saar on June 23, in which he eulogized Hitler and paid homage to him as "the man who has welded together the entire nation and saved it from threatened political collapse" (New York *Times*, June 24, 1934).

On June 25 Hess made a speech on the radio in which he stated that Hitler "is always right and he will be always right." According to Hess, Hitler was above criticism. He warned the conservatives and the monarchists not to delude themselves in the belief that the National Socialist regime would yield to a regime based on conservative and monarchist principles. He warned also "those credulous idealists . . . who gave their treasonable activities the name of 'the second revolution.' "[49]

Although events were clearly heading for a climax during the last week of June,[50] Hitler does not appear to have made up his mind about the purges until June 29.[51] Until the day before they began, he hoped that Röhm could be brought around to renounce the second revolution, stop the military activities of the SA, and return to the fold. Such hopes were not at all unreasonable, for Röhm was apparently inclined in the direction of a compromise.

By the last week of June, Röhm knew that the issue of the SA could no longer be deferred. Under the circumstances his only alternative to surrender and compromise would have been organization of an insurrection against Hitler and the army. But the futility of such a revolt must

[49] It is interesting to note that the idea of another revolution was kept alive even in this speech. "Perhaps Adolf Hitler will deem it one day to be necessary to continue the development with revolutionary means," Hess said. (*Schulthess'*, Vol. LXXV, pp. 156–160.)

[50] June 28, the army units were put on alert. At the same time the German Officers' League expelled Röhm from its ranks, and on June 29 the *Völkischer Beobachter* carried a signed article by Blomberg which indicated fairly clearly that Hitler would have the support of the army if he decided to take action against Röhm. (Bullock, 1959, p. 274; Domarus, 1962, p. 393.)

[51] In his speech to the Reichstag on July 13, Hitler admitted as much. He told the Reichstag members that a few days before June 30 he was prepared to exercise clemency. (Baynes, 1942, Vol. I, pp. 290–328. See also the accounts of Hitler's pilot, Hans Baur, 1958, p. 62; Strasser, 1938, pp. 105, 107; and Jarman, 1956, p. 162.)

have been quite obvious to Röhm, for it has been established that no SA revolt was under way in the last days of June. It may be assumed, therefore, that Röhm was inclined to compromise even though he was faced with the problem of keeping his subordinates in line.

It may be assumed also that Hitler intended to await the outcome of the Bad Wiessee conference before making up his mind about specific measures. Hitler, as the supreme SA leader, called the Bad Wiessee conference for June 30 as the annual meeting of SA leaders. It seems reasonable to assume, in view of Hitler's previous behavior during factional crises, that he intended the conference to pacify the SA leaders and to make them accept a more modest role in the National Socialist state. Hitler did not want to destroy the SA, for it was still his main weapon against the army and the conservatives; besides, he might well have provoked an insurrection and a civil war.

If Hitler had plans for the SA, however, he changed them the day before the conference. In his Reichstag speech on July 13 he asserted that he had received on that day "threatening intelligence." The convening SA leaders were confronted the next day with guns instead of speeches.

The "threatening intelligence" which reached Hitler in Godesberg on June 29 was the report that the Berlin SA had been put in a state of readiness (Heiden, 1944, pp. 756–757). A little later it was reported to him that there had been an SA meeting in Munich (Woodward & Butler, 2nd series, Vol. VI, No. 487 (July 2, 1934), pp. 781–782). In the excitement of the moment he took these as preparations for a revolt, and perhaps even a coup against himself. He saw Röhm behind these actions and jumped to the conclusion that he had been deceived. At 2 A.M. on June 30, he started for Munich to liquidate the traitors (Baur, 1958, p. 63).

The substance of the report about the Berlin SA was correct, but its interpretation was mistaken. Ernst put the Berlin SA on a state of alarm when he learned that some army units had been alerted. He assumed that this meant preparation for action against the National Socialists and the SA; naturally, he had to take the necessary countermeasures.[52] That

---

[52] SA leader Ernst's loyalty to Hitler was illustrated at the moment of his execution, when he thought he was dying for Hitler. He assumed the SS to be working with Göring on the army's side. See the explanation for the Munich SA meeting in Salomon, 1954, pp. 273–274.

foul play entered into the misunderstanding, probably on the part of Göring and Heydrich and possibly also on the part of Himmler and Goebbels, seems hardly questionable (Hoettl, 1954, pp. 27–29; Strasser, 1938, p. 102). It appears that the situation could easily have been checked by the people in Berlin before calling Hitler. This was not done, and Hitler jumped to the anticipated conclusion. It appears, therefore, that Hitler was deliberately misled the day before the conference and that he decided on violent action against the SA leaders on the spur of the moment.[53]

It may be argued, however, that the events of June, 1934, contradict the pattern of factional conflicts. Hitler did not intervene against the SA as an arbiter intent on conciliation and filled with forgiveness; he initiated the notorious blood purge. The prima facie case would certainly support this observation, but I contend that basically the pattern held true in the SA crisis, as in others.

The history of the second revolution shows quite clearly that Hitler's position in the conflict was the same as in 1925–1926, 1930, and 1932. Hitler was not identified either with the SA or with their opponents, but remained the only person to whom both sides directed their respective appeals. There is considerable evidence that Röhm believed up to the moment of his arrest that he had Hitler's confidence, and the same may be said of the opponents of the SA.[54] The SA wanted action not against Hitler but against the old order; they thought they had Hitler on their side and were willing to follow him:

the SA leaders hoped that at the Bad Wiessee reunion they would at least have an opportunity of laying their complaints before Hitler. They were in good heart because they interpreted Hitler's previous indecision to their advantage; in any event, no matter what he decided, they were determined to bow to his will. Röhm even let the Reichswehr know this.[55]

[53] Had the purge been planned in advance by Hitler, it would have been more systematically executed. But the purges were haphazard, varying greatly from one locality to another. Sporadic executions lasted well into the days of July.

[54] This has been noted repeatedly in the foregoing historical account of the crisis. That Röhm believed Hitler to be on his side is indicated in the accounts of Heiden, 1944, pp. 756–757; Strasser, 1938, p. 64, 1948, p. 185. The British Ambassador, Sir Eric Phips, reported to London on June 30 that, according to information received from von Neurath, Göring had warned about an impending SA putsch headed by Röhm. According to Göring, Röhm intended to arrest all ministers except (!) Hitler. (Woodward & Butler, 2nd series, Vol. VI, pp. 779–780.)

[55] Luetgebrune to Ernst von Salomon, Salomon, 1954, p. 273. The rank and file

Hitler followed his tactics of neutrality, keeping both sides waiting for his decision. "[He] observed the conflict, watching, waiting, speaking the language of once this, once the other group, but deciding nothing" (Görlitz & Quint, 1952, p. 399). When he decided to proceed against Röhm on June 29, he acted in fear and rage. Up to that time he believed in the possibility of a compromise between the SA and the army, and it is reasonable to assume that he would never have acted as he did had he not panicked when he received the report from Berlin about the mobilization of the Berlin SA. He thought he had been betrayed by Röhm, and in a state of rage and panic he rushed to Munich and thence to Bad Wiessee to arrest him.

The purge was neither planned nor desired by Hitler, nor was it necessary. The victims were taken completely by surprise, not even knowing what they had done to deserve their punishment. There were no signs of an SA insurrection; the SA was loyal to Hitler.[56]

Thus, the pattern of the conflict did not deviate from that of previous factional crises in any significant respect. The SA leadership was not fighting with Hitler, but was attempting to gain his support against the forces of the right virtually up to the last moment. Hitler managed to remain above the conflict by refusing to commit himself to any position and thus left all parties in doubt as to his final decision. This enabled him to retain his image of the ultimate arbiter, the person above factional quarrels who concerns himself only with the good of the

in the party approved of Hitler's actions, except in Silesia. This shows that if the revolt had been planned it could not conceivably have been directed against Hitler himself. (Greenwood, 1934, p. 305.)

[56] There are many accounts which indicate the loyalty of the SA to Hitler. "Adolf Hitler belongs to us"—this byword was to be heard in the SA quarters in the spring of 1934, according to Rauschning (1940, p. 151). Karl Ernst, SA leader in Berlin, wrote on June 3, 1934, that he would remain loyal to Hitler until death. When he died before an SS firing squad in 1934, he cried "Heil Hitler" (Strasser, *30 Juni*, p. 117). The SA leaders in Stadelheim asked for Hitler before their execution (*ibid.*, p. 135).

The SA leaders who were arrested were stunned. Hans Frank visited Röhm in his cell on June 30. Röhm was very glad to see him. "What is all this?" Röhm asked. "This morning Hitler arrested me. What is going on?" (Frank, 1953, pp. 147–149.) The SA leaders of Munich were similarly astounded when Hitler arrested them. One of them shouted at Hitler: "Are you crazy? What have you against us? How should we know that you want to depose Röhm?" (Strasser, 1938, p. 112.)

The total number killed has not been established. Estimates range from a minimum of 144 (Mau, 1953, p. 134) to 401 (Strasser, *30 Juni*, p. 90). Heiden writes of "many hundred killed" (1944, p. 769). Orb estimates their number as "more than 200." In his Reichstag speech of July 13, Hitler reported fifty-eight executions and nineteen others dead in the embroilment.

movement as a whole. This image let him survive the events of 1934 without compromising his position in the movement. Indeed, June 30 left Hitler's authority enhanced and his popularity in the movement unaffected.

The purge of the SA leadership was the culmination of the last of the factional crises in the history of the Nazi party. With the elimination of Röhm and his circle, the last of the *condottieri* were deprived of their power in the movement. The disputes and conflicts that continued in the movement after 1934 never developed into major factional disputes. After 1934 the party was too much involved in the practical tasks of domestic, international, and military reconstruction to worry about ideological questions. June, 1934, more than January, 1933, represented the end of the Kampfzeit, the time in the struggle for power that Hitler and the old guard in the party remembered with fondness and nostalgia.

EPILOGUE TO THE KAMPFZEIT

The purges of 1934 served less to destroy the movement for a second revolution than to inaugurate a new era in the history of National Socialism. The month of June did not mark the victory of the military-conservative forces over the social-revolutionaries—whatever movement may have existed for a second revolution was repudiated and dead before June 30. The SA was not destroyed to make room for some other power within the Nazi state. June, 1934, marked the victory of the totalitarian idea and its principal carrier, the SS.

The purges destroyed the last vestige of a quasi-independent power within the Nazi party; this power had existed up to June, 1934, in the SA. Hitler's assumption of the supreme SA leadership notwithstanding, the SA developed between 1930 and 1934 into a state within the shadow-state of the party. There was a paradoxically inverse relation to Hitler. Its separateness, its distinct spirit grew as it met with success. As it developed an organization comprising millions of people, a distinct *esprit de corps* evolved among its leaders. Although the SA was loyal to Hitler and its leaders never failed to express their devotion to their Führer, the leaders' loyalty was never unquestioning and unconditional, never blind and selfless. It was the kind given by members of a distinct organization to an outside authority, and as such it was always predicated on a *quid pro quo.* Theirs was a conditional loyalty that had to be constantly bolstered up by concessions, if it were to be sustained.

This was especially true of the SA leaders who had joined the SA ranks from other organizations. The former army officers and Free Corps men never completely abandoned their prior frames of reference. They did not join the SA because they were fanatical believers in the Weltanschauung, but because they saw in the SA and in Nazism a vehicle for the achievement of their traditional aims. For their loyalties to Hitler and Nazism they expected concrete rewards. Inherent in their conditional association with the party was a continuous distrust and hostility between them and the party leadership.[57]

Before the purges, the SA never accepted the totalitarian principle of absolute leadership and blind obedience. It remained a separate organization motivated by a distinct ethos. As such it could provide potentially or in fact the basis for a factional group. After the purges of 1934, the SA became a different kind of organization. It lost the leaders who had given it a distinct character; it lost its prestige and standing as the revolutionary vanguard of the Nazi movement. It became an integral part of the party—one of its service organizations, subordinated in spirit as well as in fact to the party leaders.

In July, 1934, the SA was reorganized on the basis of Hitler's twelve-point directive, the first article of which was the most significant. "I demand from the SA leader, just as from the SA man," Hitler stated, "blind obedience and unconditional discipline."[58] The SA was to be completely integrated into the party; its strength was to lie in its political tie with the party. The function of the SA was to train the spiritually and physically best-developed National Socialists.[59]

Viktor Lutze, the new chief of staff of the SA, responded in the appropriate spirit when he declared some months later that he had never spoken primarily as an SA-man but always as a National Socialist. On

---

[57] Martin Bormann expressed this distrust in one of his letters to his wife. Recalling the Pfeffer period, he wrote, "I was so terribly afraid that something bad might come from the old Free Corps and Condottieri leaders because so many of them behaved like petty kings and did not want to submit to discipline." (Trevor-Roper, 1954, p. 87.)

[58] *Trial*, Doc. SA-249, Vol. XLII, pp. 425–427. Most of the points were concerned with the private behavior of the SA man (Points 2–8), the last ones with the relation of the SA and the party.

[59] The SA was, according to the official organization manual, a training and educational instrument of the party for political and military purposes (*Trial*, Doc. 2354-PS, Vol. XXX, pp. 30, 280–285).

the position of the SA, he declared that it could never stand on the side of the movement but only within it.[60] In his directive of April, 1935, Lutze ordered that only party members were to be accepted into SA ranks (Rühle, 1935, Vol. III, pp. 77–78).

The SA declined to the point of insignificance after 1934,[61] not only because it was deprived of its ablest leaders, but because it could not compete with the SS, which assumed many of its former functions.[62] As the vanguard of the National Socialist state and as the embodiment of its spirit, the SS was a perfect totalitarian tool. It became the carrier of the National Socialist revolution, which the SA had once claimed to be, and it attracted the best talents and the most fanatical adherents to the idea of the Nazi state. Above all, the SS was identified with the person of Hitler, which had been true of the SA only sporadically. Under the circumstances, the SA rapidly dwindled and approached disintegration. Nazi leaders never allowed it to regain anything like its former strength in the years after the purges.[63]

The rise of the SS order to the point of identification with the Nazi state meant not only the decline of the SA but also the relative weakening of the power position of the party. In 1935 the party was still described as the source and the carrier of the political will of the nation, but by 1937 it became merely an instrumental link between the leader and the people.[64] The state had been conquered, the political revolution

[60] Lutze's speech of January 24, 1936, *Trial*, Doc. 2471-PS, Vol. XXX, pp. 552–569.

[61] "Under Lutze the SA became a useless civilian organization," Goebbels told Rudolf Semmler. Goebbels thought it would have been better to dissolve the SA in 1943 when Lutze died, but knowing Hitler's weakness for sentimental memories, he knew that such a decision was most unlikely. (Semmler, 1947, p. 85.) Between 1934 and 1939 the membership of the SA fell from 4½ million to 1½ million men (*Trial*, Vol. XXI, p. 121).

[62] On July 20, 1934, the SS was elevated to the status of an independent organization within the NSDAP (Verfügungen, n.d., p. 596).

[63] See Hitler's speech at the party rally of September 9, 1934, in Baynes, 1942, Vol. I, pp. 330–331, in which he attempted to divorce the SA as a whole from misdeeds of its leaders before June, 1934.

In a speech on October 17, 1935, Goebbels warned against the mistake of regarding the SA as superfluous. Indeed, he said, "the strongest power in the movement is the SA." (*Trial*, Doc. 3211-PS, Vol. XXXII, pp. 46–47.) In July, 1934, Hess gave a similar warning to those who tried to defame the SA (*ibid.*, Doc. 3054-PS, Vol. XXXI, pp. 524–536).

[64] Rühle, 1935, Vol. III, p. 64; Vol. V, p. 111. In this semiofficial documentary history of the National Socialist state after 1935 the party was frequently not even accorded a separate section. See also Peterson, 1966, pp. 172–192.

was ended, and Hitler paid less and less attention to party matters.[65] From his beginnings as an agitator and party leader, he became a statesman preoccupied with international and military problems.

After the mid-1930's the membership of Hitler's inner circle ceased to be exclusively or even primarily party leaders.[66] They were mostly excluded from decision-making and their encounters with Hitler were severely limited.[67] Hitler appeared only infrequently in a representative capacity before party rallies, and after 1936 even the latter lost much of their luster and significance.[68] The party, with its often corrupt, uneducated, and mostly unspectacular leaders, could not compete with the SS, which gradually took over most of the functions of the party in the totalitarian state. After 1934 it was more and more often the SS that was the principal training ground for the new elite; it became the principal avenue to power. It was the SS which became the carrier of the spiritual revolution, the instrument for the realization of the ideal Nazi community. Whereas the party was bogged down in the administration of daily affairs and more and more identified with the imperfect present, the SS was envisaged as the vanguard of the perfect future. Whereas the party gave the impression of being a group of quarreling petty bureaucrats concerned with their own advancement and privileges, the SS was looked upon as the epitome of unity, discipline, revolutionary ardor, sacrifice, and selfless devotion to the leader and the idea of the National Socialist state.

The synchronization of all aspects of life that had begun in 1933 proceeded with greater intensity after 1934.[69] Its beneficiary and the princi-

[65] "I've totally lost sight of the organization of the party," said Hitler in 1941. "When I find myself confronted by one or the other of these achievements, I say to myself: 'by God, how that has developed!'" (1953, p. 125; see also Semmler, 1947, p. 86; Buchheim *et al.*, 1960, pp. 10–11; *Trial*, Doc. 3163-PS, Vol. XXXII, pp. 41–42.)

[66] From 1934 on many party leaders heard of great decisions only on the radio (Dietrich, 1955, p. 46).

[67] See Dietrich, 1955, pp. 45–46; Rosenberg's memo to Hitler, December 18, 1933, in Seraphim, 1956, p. 129; Kersten, 1952, p. 62.

[68] The last party rally in Nuremberg was held in 1938. During the war years Hitler usually restricted his party talks to his November and February speeches to the Old Fighters. See Frank, 1953, p. 298; Dietrich, 1955, pp. 45–46.

[69] In August, 1934, Hindenburg died, and Hitler became the head of state as well as the head of government. In the same year the NSBO (National Socialist Industrial Cell Organization) was developed, and its tasks and competences were transferred to the German Workers Front. In 1935 the Stahlhelm was dissolved, and in the summer of 1936 the personal union of the Chief of the German Police and the Reichsführer of the SS was accomplished. In December, 1937, Hjalmar Schacht resigned

pal carrier of the idea of the emerging totalitarian state was the SS. After 1934 the SS penetrated all spheres of activity, a state of affairs that has led several writers to refer to the Third Reich after 1934 as the "SS state." Despite the accumulation of enormous powers, however, the SS never threatened Hitler's leadership. There was not the inverse relation between the powers of the organization and the principle of absolute leadership that existed between the SA and Hitler. The growth of the power of the SS represented the success of the totalitarian idea, personified in Hitler.

The SS was based on the sanctity of orders regardless of substance; its code was unconditional obedience.[70] In their oath, SS men swore unqualified loyalty to the person of Adolf Hitler.[71] The SS was an organization of men who broke with all traditions and who followed their superiors blindly without questions or reservations[72]; it was the ideal political expression of the Nazi state. The motto of its members, "My honor is my loyalty," revealed the emptiness of their fanaticism and made them ideal mercenaries of the totalitarian leader.

The character of the SS was excellently outlined by Himmler in a speech delivered in Munich on March 10, 1934. He reminded his audience of the principles underlying the organization of the SS:

In years past we have never forgotten the three major virtues: loyalty, which comes from the heart; obedience, which never asks why; and comraderie, which means all for one and one for all. We want to be, as long as we live, simple and honest soldiers. We want to fight and be disciplined when Adolf Hitler so orders. [*Schulthess'*, Vol. LXXV, p. 92.]

With the progressive inculcation of the SS virtues into the party, the period of substantive discussions about the nature and goal of National

as Minister of Economics. Most of his powers were transferred to Göring, the director of the Four-Year Plan. In February, 1938, Hitler assumed the office of the Commander-in-Chief of the Armed Forces and abolished the Ministry of War. In 1943 Himmler became the Minister of the Interior.

[70] Himmler, "Das Schwarze Korps," *Nationalsozialistisches Jahrbuch*, 1937, pp. 255–256. On the SS see Görlitz, 1960; Neusüss-Hunkel, 1956; Reitlinger, 1956; Paetel, 1953.

The SS was not burdened by any spiritual or political tradition but was motivated only by its loyalty to the Führer (Buchheim, 1958, p. 16).

[71] See the SS oath in *Trial*, Doc. 744-D, Vol. XXXV, pp. 475–476, and Doc. 3429-PS, Vol. XXXII, p. 284.

[72] The samples of these attitudes are found in two of Himmler's speeches—his address to the officer corps of September 7, 1940, *Trial*, Doc. 1918-PS, Vol. XXIX, pp. 98–110, and his speech in Pognan on October 4, 1943, *Trial*, Doc. 1919-PS, Vol. XXIX, pp. 110–173.

Socialism was over. The task of the coming years was not to theorize about ideals, but to establish conditions of stability and order by being loyal, obedient, and self-sacrificing.[73] The future lay with the functionaries, with the technicians of power, who saw their tasks limited to the "execution of orders at any price" (Frank, 1953, pp. 246–247). The enthusiasts of the Kampfzeit who were unable to make this transition were slowly pushed to the sidelines as the "Order State" took over.

[73] See Hitler's proclamation to the Nuremberg rally, September 6, 1934, "Aufklärungs-und-Redner-Informations-material der Reichspropagandaleitung," Lieferung No. 10, October, 1934. Stanford University, Hoover Library Special Collection.

CONCLUSION

Toward a Theory of Factional Conflicts

THIS study has attempted to demonstrate the significance of the charismatic type of legitimacy for the pattern of factionalism in the Nazi party. Charismatic legitimacy made Hitler the sole source of authority and the only point of cohesion in the otherwise heterogeneous movement. Hitler's charisma elevated him above factional conflicts and allowed him to assume the position of broker, arbiter, and judge. Factions justified their existence by claiming to be Hitler's representatives, which meant that they organized not to challenge Hitler's authority but to gain his support against rival factions. Factional conflicts took place on the secondary levels of leadership; the charismatic leader as the source of legitimacy remained above conflict.

Ideological issues that have split up communist and socialist movements during the past century presented no danger to the unity of the Nazi movement, based on the Weltanschauung and charisma. Factions in the Hitler movement could champion diverse programmatic courses within the framework of the esoteric Weltanschauung and its representative, Hitler. Thus, factions advocating differing programs were not incompatible with either the Weltanschauung or the source of legitimacy. They did not impair the principal focus of cohesion of the group and hence could safely be tolerated. The existence of factions with radically different programmatic orientations during the Kampfzeit preserved the heterogeneity of the movement, which enabled it to appeal to all classes and to the most diverse interests.

The dependent position of the factions exposed them to manipulation by the charismatic leader. Since factional conflicts on the lower levels served several useful functions (such as dividing potential challengers, broadening the appeal of the movement to diverse classes, and enhancing the importance of the charismatic leader as the sole point of unity), Hitler not only tolerated them, but even encouraged their continued existence. The most noticeable tactics utilized by Hitler to this end were his organizational devices (such as assigning both exclusive and overlapping jurisdictions), his reluctance to commit himself to any point of view, and his proclivity to avoid making decisions, thus perpetuating confusion among his subordinates about his intentions and ultimate course of action. His refusal to get involved in factional disputes reinforced his authority and prestige as the man interested only in the ultimate issues of the Weltanschauung and in the continued unity of the movement.

It was only when a faction challenged or appeared to challenge his ultimate authority that Hitler reluctantly intervened. His mediation was always decisive for the future of the faction even though hesitatingly made and postponed to the last moment. Once Hitler disowned a faction,, he deprived it of its legitimacy—the faction could no longer claim to be his representative or exploit his charisma. At such moments factional leaders in opposition to Hitler found themselves isolated; their support evaporated, and Hitler emerged with his authority unimpaired and with the unity of the movement preserved.

Although it is impossible in the absence of other case studies on factionalism in charismatically legitimated groups to demonstrate that the pattern of factionalism observed in the Nazi party would appear also in other charismatic groups, nevertheless a few strikingly parallel cases may be cited to illustrate this proposition. President Sukarno of Indonesia, whose rule has been frequently characterized as charismatic, has always sought to balance the factional forces of the army and the Communist party around him without identifying himself with either. The two factions have tried in vain to have Sukarno take a position. At the time of the abortive uprising, Colonel Untung could not "get President Sukarno to the microphone *to lend legitimacy to their efforts*" (Leifer, 1965, pp. 13–15; italics added), which was an important reason for the failure of his group. The two charismatic leaders of modern India, Gandhi and Nehru, pursued similar tactics when they managed to relate to all factions within the heterogeneous Congress movement (Goyal & Wallace, 1964, pp. 180–201). Nehru was known to vacillate and refuse to take a position because by remaining at the center "he could both create and keep under control group rivalries" (Krishna, 1963, p. 11). George Washington's relation with factional leaders paralleled those above, although not by conscious design. Washington, who was the primary agent holding the Union together,[1] refused to align himself with any of the competing factions until the last years of his presidency. "Until Jefferson had withdrawn each party had been represented at court and could have a hearing" (Charles, 1956, p. 42). Washington's prestige "enhanced the importance of those believed to be in his confidence"; thus Hamilton could carry out his program without interference, for an attack on him would unavoidably have included the President. Finally, Washington's isolation and his reluctance to make decisions parallel the behavior of charismatic leaders (Charles, 1956, pp. 37–51). Stalin, although not a charismatic leader, approached through the "cult of personality" a personal autocracy analogous to charismatic leadership. By the 1930's factionalism in the CPSU (Communist Party of the Soviet Union) approached the character of Nazi factional conflicts:

The struggle that had been going on since the autumn of 1933 in the ranks of the Party leaders differed very greatly from similar conflicts in the past. Whereas formerly all forms of opposition had been opposition *against* Stalin and for his removal from the post of Party Chief, there was now no longer any question of such removal. The groupings were now not for or against Stalin. Everyone emphasized tirelessly his devotion to Stalin. It was rather *a fight for influence over Stalin,* a fight for his soul so to speak. The question as to the group for which he would ultimately declare himself at the decisive moment remained open, and since the direction of policy in the immediate future depended on Stalin's decision, each group tried to win him over to his side. [Nicolaevsky, 1965, p. 44.]

Once his leadership was assured and recognized, Stalin began to employ Hitlerian tactics toward his quarreling lieutenants. He "encourage[d] rivalry among his immediate lieutenants, well aware that such

[1] "The influence of Washington himself, from the establishment of the new government to his death, is of an importance which all who have studied the period have acknowledged. Affection for him and complete trust in him were at times during this period probably the only sentiments which were shared without important reservations by the mass of the people throughout the country. These sentiments were called into service to support government policy at every important crisis from 1793 on, and provided on these occasions the most important check on criticism of the government's course." (Charles, 1956, pp. 37–38; cf. also Lipset, 1963, pp. 18–23.)

rivalry presented less threat to himself than would a solid band of men who saw eye to eye" (Schapiro, 1960, p. 506). He also realized the importance of not identifying himself with any of the warring factions too closely. Instead, he maneuvered between them and played the part of the supreme arbiter (Leonhard, 1962, p. 35).

The significance of the type of legitimacy to the nature of factional conflicts suggests the possibility of a typology of factionalism to complement the typology of groups. Although the contribution of sociologists and social psychologists to intragroup conflicts has been most significant in the field of small group studies, certain analyses have been advanced that may be utilized as points of departure for a political concept of faction. Groups have been defined by sociologists by the interdependence of their members, which becomes both the source of cohesion and the potential source of disruption (French, 1941, p. 368). "Interdependence" implies that every member is dependent on the others in the group, and the cumulative realization of this dependency is a centripetal force that creates and maintains the group. Dependence, however, is also a potential source of frustration for the individual, and as such it can cause intragroup differences that may or may not disrupt the group. Intragroup divisions are in this sense inherent in groups, although their particular manifestations will depend on the nature and extent of individual dissatisfactions.

The theoretical model of factionalism would have to assume a continuum in which a group based on minimal segmental participation is at one extreme and an ideal totalitarian group based on complete identification is at the other. Both extremes would logically deny the existence of factions that could exist only on the continuum—this is not a contradiction to the original statement that factions are inherent characteristics of groups, for groups could only exist *on* the continuum, not at the extremes. Both extremes destroy the concept of the group; at one extreme the group is destroyed in favor of individual members, at the other extreme the individual member is destroyed in favor of the group. Factions assume the existence of both individuals and the collectivity; hence they cannot exist where one or the other is missing. Thus, in a group with the least conceivable interdependence, frustrations would be minimized to the extent that no differences could arise among the members. Similarly, factions would be impossible in an ideal totalitarian group based on total identification with the leaders because they would by definition disrupt the group.

On the continuum, however, one may chart certain relations of factions *vis-à-vis* groups. To the extent that groups involve a greater part of the devotion of each member and to the extent that each member becomes dependent on his fellow members, factions become more clearcut and potentially more disruptive for the group. The tighter the group cohesion, the more incompatible are factions with the group; in a group based on monolithic unity, factions are identical with party splits.[2]

This simple model based on the degree of group cohesion becomes more complicated when one considers the nature of group cohesion. If the degree of cohesion were the only determinant of factionalism, there would be no reason to expect wide variations between various Communist and Nazi factions. But the differences between Communist and Nazi factionalisms are due to the different nature of their cohesion: the cohesion of Communist groups is based on ideology, the cohesion of Nazi groups on the charisma of the leader. Communist leaders always justify themselves by claiming to be the correct interpreters of the Marxist ideology, and on this basis they claim the loyalty of their followers. In Nazism the leader and the Weltanschauung were by definition one; hence there was no need for the leader to claim the loyalties of his followers on any other than a personal basis.

The different relation between leadership and ideology in the Communist and Nazi movements is of utmost importance for factionalism. Factions are based on some issue of ideological importance. In the Communist movement an ideological issue raises a question of loyalty that must be defined in ideological terms. But in any totalitarian movement based on an ideology, disagreements about the ideology are automatically disloyal acts and, therefore, illegitimate. Thus, factions in Communist movements cannot claim the only possible legitimizing basis, and their existence is incompatible with the group as a whole (Djilas, 1957, pp. 75ff).

---

[2] "In groups that appeal only to a peripheral part of their members' personality, or, to use Parsons's terminology, in groups in which relations are functionally specific and affectively neutral, conflicts are apt to be less sharp and violent than in groups wherein ties are diffuse and affective, engaging the total personality of their members. In effect, this suggests that conflicts in groups such as Rotary Clubs or Chambers of Commerce are likely to be less violent than in groups such as religious sects or radical parties of the Communist type." (Coser, 1956, pp. 68–69; see also Coleman, 1957, p. 3.)

The leadership principle of Nazism, on the other hand, permitted factions because programmatic disagreements did not necessarily involve the question of loyalty. Loyalty accrued to the person of the leader, who was identified only with the absolute Idea, not with any particular ideology. This allowed considerable programmatic latitude for the factions because programs were subordinate to the leader and the Idea. When one considers the nature as well as the degree of cohesion, it becomes clear that factions are not necessarily incompatible with a totalitarian group based on charismatic legitimacy because they do not challenge the principle of absolute leadership. They did become incompatible with Nazi totalitarianism, however, when they challenged this principle (Neumann, 1965, p. 74).

The nature of group cohesion, or the principle of legitimacy, is, therefore, the key to the pattern of factionalism in a group. In a non-totalitarian group the principle of legitimacy is pluralistic—i.e., based on segmental participation—and factions can exist without destroying the group. In a totalitarian movement the principle of legitimacy is monistic —i.e., based on an almost total identification—and factions can exist only if they do not attack the principle of legitimacy. In a charismatic totalitarian movement, factions do not necessarily attack the principle of legitimacy; in an ideological totalitarian movement, they necessarily do so.

These concluding observations need to be investigated in further studies. I have analyzed the nature of factionalism in only one charismatic movement. A theory of factional behavior and factionalism as such will have to await further studies of factionalism in totalitarian as well as non-totalitarian political organizations. The prospect of such a theory is exciting because the character of factional conflicts, conditioned as they are by the nature of legitimacy, may provide significant indications about the nature of political organization. In this manner, a theory of factional behavior may lead to analyses of political groups that will produce a new typology of political parties. Finally, a more systematic analysis of factional conflicts may throw new light on the concept of legitimacy by providing an empirical index that suggests new typologies of authority.

BIBLIOGRAPHY AND INDEX

Bibliography

Abel, Theodore. *Why Hitler Came into Power.* New York: Prentice-Hall, 1938.

Apter, David E., ed. *Ideology and Discontent.* Glencoe, Ill.: Free Press, 1964.

Arendt, Hannah. *The Origins of Totalitarianism,* 2nd ed. New York: Harcourt (Meridian), 1958.

Ascher, Abraham, and Günther Lewy. "National Bolshevism in Weimar Germany," *Social Research,* XXIII (Winter, 1956), 450–480.

Aufklärungs- und Redner-Informationsmaterial der Reichspropagandaleitung: Rechtswesen, Allgemeines. Stanford University: Hoover Library Special File.

Barbu, Zevedei. *Democracy and Dictatorship: Their Psychology and Patterns of Life.* New York: Grove, 1956.

Baumont, Maurice, John H. E. Fried, and Edmond Vermeil, eds. *The Third Reich.* New York: Praeger, 1955.

Baur, Hans. *Hitler's Pilot.* London: Frederick Muller, 1958.

Baynes, Norman H., ed. *The Speeches of Adolf Hitler,* Vol. I. London: Oxford University Press, 1942.

Bell, Daniel. *The End of Ideology: On the Exhaustion of Political Ideas in the Fifties,* rev. ed. New York: Collier, 1961.

Blase, Alexander, ed. *Das Dritte Reich.* Hanover: Verlag für Literatur und Zeitgeschehen, 1963.

Bölcke, Rolf. "Die Spaltung der Nationalsozialisten," *Die Tat,* XXII (August, 1930), 357–367.

Bracher, Karl D., Wolfgang Sauer, and Gerhard Schulz. *Die Nationalsozialistische Machtergreifung: Studien zur Errichtung des totalitären Herrschaftssystems in Deutschland 1933–1934.* Cologne & Opladen: Westdeutscher, 1960.

Bramstedt, Ernst K. *Dictatorship and Political Police.* New York: Oxford University Press, 1945.

———. "Joseph Goebbels and National Socialist Propaganda, 1926–1939: Some Aspects," *Australian Outlook,* VIII (June, 1954), 65–77.

Broszat, Martin. "Die völkische Ideologie und der Nationalsozialismus," *Deutsche Rundschau,* LXXXIV (January, 1958), 53–68.

———. *Der Nationalsozialismus.* Stuttgart: Deutsche Verlags-Anstalt, 1960.

Buchheim, Hans. *Das Dritte Reich.* Munich: Kösel, 1958.

———, Edith Eucken-Erdsiek, Gert Buchheit, and H. G. Adler. *Der Führer ins Nichts.* Rastatt: Grote'sche, 1960.

Bullock, Alan. *Hitler: A Study in Tyranny,* 4th ptg. Long Acre, London: Odhams, 1959.

153

Charles, Joseph. *The Origins of the American Party System.* Williamsburg, Va.: Institute of Early American History and Culture, 1956.

Coleman, James S. *Community Conflict.* New York: Free Press, 1957.

Coser, Lewis A. *The Function of Social Conflict.* Glencoe, Ill.: Free Press, 1956.

Czech-Jochberg, Erich. *Adolf Hitler und sein Stab.* Oldenburg: Gerhard Stalling, 1933.

David, Claude. *L'Allemagne de Hitler.* Paris: Presses Universitaires de France, 1954.

Davies, James C. "Charisma in the 1952 Campaign," *American Political Science Review,* XLVIII (December, 1954), 1083–1102.

Dietrich, Otto. *12 Jahre mit Hitler.* Munich: Isar, 1955.

Djilas, Milovan. *The New Class: An Analysis of the Communist System.* New York: Praeger, 1957.

Documents on German Foreign Policy 1918–1945, Series C, Vols. I–VI. London: H.M.S.O., 1949–1951.

Domarus, Max. *Hitler: Reden und Proklamationen. 1932–1945,* Vol. I. Neustadt on the Aisch: Schmidt, 1962.

Drage, Charles. *The Amiable Prussian.* London: Anthony Blond, 1958.

Drexler, Anton. *Mein Politisches Erwachen,* 4th ed. Munich: Deutscher Volksverlag, 1937.

Engelbrechten, Julius Karl von. *Eine braune Armee entsteht.* Munich: Franz Eher, 1940.

Fagen, Richard. "Charismatic Authority and the Leadership of Fidel Castro," *Western Political Quarterly,* XVIII (June, 1965), 275–284.

Fest, Joachim. *Das Gesicht des Dritten Reiches.* Munich: R. Piper, 1963.

Forsthoff, Ernst, ed. *Deutsche Geschichte von 1918 bis 1938 in Dokumenten,* 3rd ed. Stuttgart: Alfred Kroener, 1938.

Frank, Hans. *Im Angesicht des Galgens.* Munich & Gräfelfing: Friedrich Alfred Beck, 1953.

Franz, Georg. "Munich: Birthplace and Center of the National Socialist German Workers Party," *Journal of Modern History,* XXIX (December, 1957), 326–328.

Franz-Willing, Georg. *Die Hitlerbewegung: Der Ursprung 1919–1922.* Hamburg & Berlin: R. v. Decker's Verlag G. Schenk, 1962.

French, John R. P., Jr. "The Disruption and Cohesion of Groups," *Journal of Abnormal and Social Psychology,* XXXVI (July, 1941), 362–377.

Frick, Wilhelm. *Die nationalsozialisten im Reichstag, 1924–1931.* Munich: Franz Eher, 1932.

Friedrich, Carl J. "Political Leadership and the Problem of Charismatic Power," *Journal of Politics,* XXIII (February, 1961), 3–24.

―――, and Zbigniew Brzezinski. *Totalitarian Dictatorship and Autocracy,* 2nd ed. Cambridge, Mass.: Harvard University Press, 1965.

Gebhardt, Bruno. *Handbuch der deutschen Geschichte, Die Zeit der Weltkriege* by Karl D. Erdmann, rev. ed. Vol. IV, Stuttgart: Union, 1960.

Germino, Dante L. *The Italian Fascist Party in Power.* Minneapolis: University of Minnesota Press, 1959.

―――. "The Revival of Political Theory," *Journal of Politics,* XXV (August, 1963), 437–460.

Gerth, Hans. "The Nazi Party, Its Leadership and Composition," *American Journal of Sociology,* XLV (January, 1940), 517–541.

Gilbert, G. M. *Nuremberg Diary.* New York: New American Library (Signet), 1961.

Gisevius, Hans Bernd. *Adolf Hitler: Versuch einer Deutung.* Munich: Rutten & Loening, 1963.

Glum, Friedrich. *Der Nationalsozialismus.* Munich: C. H. Beck, 1962.

Goebbels, Joseph. *Die zweite Revolution: Briefe an Zeitgenossen.* Zwickau (Sax.): Streiter, n.d.

————. *Vom Kaiserhof zur Reichskanzlei.* Munich: Franz Eher, 1937.

————. *Tagebuch.* See Heiber, ed.

Görlitz, Walter. *Die Waffen-SS.* Berlin & Grunwald: Arami, 1960.

————, and Herbert A. Quint. *Adolf Hitler: Eine Biographie.* Stuttgart: Stein-grüben, 1952.

Goyal, O. P., and Paul Wallace. "The Congress Party—A Conceptual Study," *India Quarterly,* XX (June, 1964), 180–201.

Grebing, Helga. *Der Nationalsozialismus: Ursprung und Wesen.* Munich: Isar, 1959.

Greenwood, H. Powys. *The German Revolution.* London: Routledge, 1934.

Groth, Alexander J. "The 'Isms' in Totalitarianism," *American Political Science Review,* LVIII (December, 1964), 888–901.

Hale, Oron James. "Gottfried Feder Calls Hitler to Order: An Unpublished Letter on Nazi Party Affairs," *Journal of Modern History,* XXX (December, 1958), 358–362.

Hanfstängl, Ernst. *Hitler: The Missing Years.* London: Eyre & Spottiswoode, 1957.

Hanna, Willard A. *Eight Nation Makers: Southeast Asia's Charismatic Statesmen.* New York: St. Martin's, 1964.

Heberle, Rudolf. *From Democracy to Nazism.* Baton Rouge: Louisiana State University Press, 1945.

Heiber, Helmut, ed. *Das Tagebuch von Joseph Goebbels 1925/26.* Stuttgart: Deutsche Verlags-Anstalt, n.d.

Heiden, Konrad. *A History of National Socialism.* New York: Knopf, 1935.

————. *Der Führer.* Boston: Houghton, 1944.

Hitler, Adolf. *Mein Kampf,* editorial sponsors John Chamberlain *et al.* New York: Reynal, 1939.

————. *Hitler's Secret Conversations 1941–1944.* New York: Farrar, 1953.

————. *Hitlers Zweites Buch: Ein Dokument aus dem Jahr 1928.* Stuttgart: Deutsche Verlags-Anstalt, 1961.

————. *Speeches.* See Baynes, ed.

Hoettl, Wilhelm. *The Secret Front.* New York: Praeger, 1954.

Holborn, Hajo. "Origins and Political Character of Nazi Ideology," *Political Science Quarterly,* LXXIX (December, 1964), 542–554.

Huntington, Samuel P. "Conservatism as an Ideology," *American Political Science Review,* LI (June, 1957), 454–473.

Jarman, T. L. *The Rise and Fall of Nazi Germany.* New York: New York University Press, 1956.

Jochmann, Werner. *Nationalsozialismus und Revolution: Ursprung und Geschichte der* NSDAP *in Hamburg 1922–1933. Dokumente.* Frankfort on the Main: Europäische, 1963.

Kelley, Douglas M. *22 Cells in Nuremberg.* New York: Greenberg, 1947.

Kersten, Felix. *Totenkopf und Treue.* Hamburg: Robert Mölich, 1952.

King, C. Wendell. *Social Movements in the United States.* New York: Random House, 1956.

Klemperer, Klemens von. "Towards a Fourth Reich? The History of National Bolshevism in Germany," *Review of Politics,* XIII (April, 1951), 191–210.

Koehl, Robert. "Feudal Aspects of National Socialism," *American Political Science Review,* LIV (December, 1960), 921–933.

Koestler, Arthur. *The Invisible Writing.* New York: Macmillan, 1954.

Kogon, Eugen. *The Theory and Practice of Hell.* Berkley: Medallion, 1960.

Kolnai, Aurel. *The War Against the West.* New York: Viking, 1938.

Krebs, Albert. *Tendenzen und Gestalten der* NSDAP. Stuttgart: Deutsche Verlags-Anstalt, 1959.

Krishna, B. "Nehru's India and the Kamaraj Plan," *Eastern World,* XVII (December, 1963), 11–12, 24–26.

Kühnl, Reinhard. "Zur Programmatik der Nationalsozialistischen Linken: Das Strasser-Programm von 1925/26," *Vierteljahrshefte für Zeitgeschichte*, XIV (July, 1966), 315–333.

Leifer, Michael. "The Non-Toppling of Sukarno," *Venture*, XVII (December, 1965), 13–15.

Leonhard, Wolfgang. *The Kremlin Since Stalin*. New York: Praeger, 1962.

Lipset, Seymour Martin. *Political Man*. New York: Doubleday, 1960.

——. *The First New Nation*. New York: Basic Books, 1963.

Loewenstein, Karl. *Hitler's Germany*. New York: Macmillan, 1939.

——. "The Role of Ideologies in Political Change," *International Social Science Bulletin*, V (1953), 51–74.

Los Angeles *Times*, 1965.

Lüdecke, Kurt G. W. *I Knew Hitler*. London: Jarrolds, 1938.

Mannheim, Karl. *Ideology and Utopia*. New York: Harcourt (Harvest), 1936.

Manvell, Roger, and Heinrich Fraenkel. *Dr. Goebbels: His Life and Death*. New York: Simon, 1960.

Mau, Hermann. "Die 'Zweite Revolution'—der 30 Juni 1934," *Vierteljahrshefte für Zeitgeschichte*, I (April, 1953), 119–137.

Maurois, André. *A History of France*, trans. by H. L. Binse. New York: Grove Press (Evergreen), 1960.

Meisel, James H. *The Myth of the Ruling Class*. Ann Arbor: University of Michigan Press, 1958.

Meissner, Otto. *Staatssekretär*, 3rd ptg. Hamburg: Hoffmann & Campe, 1950.

Metzger, Walter P. "Ideology and the Intellectual: A Study of Thorstein Veblen," *Philosophy of Science*, XVI (April, 1949), 125–133.

Michaelis, Herbert, and Ernst Schraepler, eds. *Ursachen und Folgen: Vom deutschen Zusammenbruch 1918 und 1945 bis zur staatlichen Neuordnung Deutschlands in der Gegenwart*, Vol. III, *Der Weg in die Weimarer Republik*. Berlin: Dokumenten, Dr. Herbert Wendler, n.d.

Miltenberg, Weigand von (pseud. of Herbert Blank). *Adolf Hitler Wilhelm III*. Berlin: Ernst Rowohlt, 1931.

Mohler, Armin. *Die Konservative Revolution in Deutschland 1918–1932*. Stuttgart: Friedrich Vorwerk, 1950.

National Archives, Washington, D.C. *Captured German Documents Filmed at Berlin*. Microfilming Program at the Berlin Document Center. American Historical Association Microcopy No. T-580.

Nationalsozialistisches Jahrbuch 1927–1944. Munich: Franz Eher.

Neumann, Franz. *Behemoth*. New York: Oxford University Press, 1944.

Neumann, Sigmund. *Permanent Revolution*, 2nd ed. New York: Praeger, 1965.

Neusüss-Hunkel, Ermenhild von. *Die SS*. Hanover & Frankfort on the Main: Norddeutsche, O. Goedel, 1956.

New York *Times*, 1934, 1962.

Nicolaevsky, Boris. *Power and the Soviet Elite*. New York: Praeger, 1965.

Oehme, Walter, and Kurt Caro. *Kommt "das Dritte Reich"?* Berlin: Ernst Rowohlt, 1930.

Olden, Rudolf. *Hitler*. New York: Covici-Friede, 1936.

Orb, Heinrich. *13 Jahre Machtrausch*, 2nd ed. Olten: Otto Walter, 1945.

Paetel, Karl O. "Der deutsche Nationalbolschewismus 1918–1932, Ein Bericht," *Aussenpolitik*, III (April, 1952), 229–242.

——, "The Rule of the Black Order: A Typology of the SS," *Diogenes*, III (Summer, 1953), 71–88.

Peterson, E. N. "The Bureaucracy and the Nazi Party," *The Review of Politics*, XXVIII (April, 1966), 172–192.

Posse, Ernst H. *Die politischen Kampfbünde Deutschlands.* Berlin: Junker & Düennhaupt, 1931.
Ranney, Austin, and Willmoore Kendall. *Democracy and the American Party System.* New York: Harcourt, 1956.
Ratnam, K. J. "Charisma and Political Leadership," *Political Studies,* XII (October, 1964), 341–354.
Rauschning, Hermann. *Die Revolution des Nihilismus.* Zurich & New York: Europa, 1938.
———. *Gespräche mit Hitler.* New York: Europa, 1940.
Reed, Douglas. *Nemesis? The Story of Otto Strasser.* London: Jonathan Cape, 1940.
———. *The Prisoner of Ottawa: Otto Strasser.* London: Jonathan Cape, 1953.
Reichmann, Eva G. *Hostages of Civilization.* Boston: Beacon, 1951.
Reitlinger, Gerald. *The SS: Alibi of a Nation 1922–1945.* London: Heinemann, 1956.
Röhm, Ernst. Addresses and essays. Hoover Library Special File.
———. *Die Geschichte eines Hochverräters.* Munich: Franz Eher, 1928.
Rose, Richard, ed. *Studies in British Politics.* New York: St. Martin's, 1966.
Rosenberg, Alfred. *Das Wesensgefüge des Nationalsozialismus.* Munich: Franz Eher, 1932.
———. *Der Mythus der 20. Jahrhunderts.* Munich: Hoheneichen, 1939.
———. *Letzte Aufzeichnungen.* Göttingen: Plesse, 1955.
———. *Politische Tagebuch.* See Seraphim, ed.
Rossbach, Gerhard. *Mein Weg durch die Zeit: Erinnerungen und Bekenntnisse.* Weilburg on the Lahn: Vereinigte Weilburger Buchdruckverein, 1950.
Rühle, Gerd. *Das Dritte Reich: Dokumentarische Darstellung des Aufbaues der Nation,* Vols. III, V. Berlin: Hummel, 1935.
Salomon, Ernst von. *The Answers of Ernst von Salomon,* trans. by Constantine Fitzgibbon. London: Putnam, 1954.
Schäfer, Wolfgang. *NSDAP: Entwicklung und Struktur der Staatspartei des dritten Reiches.* Hanover & Frankfort on the Main: Norddeutsche, O. Goedel, 1957.
Schapiro, Leonard. *The Communist Party of the Soviet Union.* New York: Random House, 1960.
Schapke, Richard. *Die Schwarze Front: Von den Zielen und Aufgaben und vom Kampfe der deutschen Revolution.* Leipzig: Wolfgang Richard Lindner, 1932.
Schulthess' Europäischer Geschichtskalender. Munich: C. H. Beck'sche.
Schumann, Hans-Gerd. *Nationalsozialismus und Gewerkschaftsbewegung.* Hanover & Frankfort on the Main: Norddeutsche, O. Goedel, 1958.
Semmler, Rudolf. *Goebbels—The Man Next to Hitler.* London: Westhous, 1947.
Seraphim, Hans-Günther, ed. *Das politische Tagebuch Alfred Rosenbergs.* Göttingen: Musterschmidt, 1956.
Shils, Edward. "Charisma, Order, and Status," *American Sociological Review,* XXX (April, 1965), 199–213.
Shirer, William L. *Berlin Diary.* New York: Knopf (Popular Library), 1961.
Springer, Hildegard, ed. *Es Sprach Hans Fritzsche.* Stuttgart: Thiele, 1949.
Stanford University. Hoover Library Microfilm Collection. *Documents from the N.S.D.A.P Main Archives.*
Stephan, Werner. "Grenzen des Nationalsozialistischen Vormarsches," *Zeitschrift für Politik,* XXI (December, 1931), 570–578.
Stern, Fritz. *The Politics of Cultural Despair.* Berkeley & Los Angeles: University of California Press, 1961.
Strasser, Georg. *Freiheit und Brot,* 3rd ed. Berlin: Kampfverlag, n.d.
———. *Kampf um Deutschland: Reden und Aufsätze eines Nationalsozialisten.* Munich: Franz Eher, 1932.
Strasser, Otto. *30 Juni.* Prague: Heinrich Grunov, n.d.
———. *Ministersessel oder Revolution,* 3rd ed. Berlin: Nationale Sozialist, n.d.

————. *Die deutsche Bartholomäusnacht,* 7th ed. Prague, Zurich, Brussels: Dritte Front, 1938.

————. *L'Aigle prussien sur l'Allemagne.* Montreal & New York: Valizuette, Brentano, 1941.

————. *Hitler und Ich.* Constance: Asmus, 1948.

————, and Michael Stern. *Flight from Terror.* New York: McBride, 1943.

Sündermann, Helmut. *Das dritte Reich.* Leoni on the Starnberger Sea: Druffel, 1964.

Szende, Paul. "Die Krise der mitteleuropäischen Revolution: Ein massenpsychologischer Versuch," *Archiv für Sozialwissenschaft und Sozialpolitik,* XLVII (1920–1921), 337–375.

Die Tat, 1930.

Thorwald, Jürgen. *Wen Sie Verderben Wollen.* Stuttgart: Steingrüben, 1952.

Thyssen, Fritz. *I Paid Hitler.* New York & Toronto: Farrer, 1941.

Trevor-Roper, Hugh R. *The Last Days of Hitler.* New York: Macmillan, 1947.

————, ed. *The Bormann Letters.* London: Weidenfeld & Nicholson, 1954.

Trial of the Major War Criminals before the International Military Tribunal. Vols. I–XXIII, *Proceedings;* Vols. XXIV–XLII, *Documents in Evidence.* Nuremberg, 1947–1949. "This volume is published in accordance with the direction of the International Military Tribunal by the Secretariat of the Tribunal, under the jurisdiction of the Allied Control Authority for Germany."

University of California, Los Angeles, Department of Special Collections. *Documents from the NSDAP Main Archives.*

Verfügungen/Anordnungen/Bekanntgaben, Vols. I–III. Munich: Franz Eher.

Völkischer Beobachter, 1925–1926, 1932.

Vogelsang, Thilo. "Zur Politik Schleichers Gegenüber der NSDAP, 1932," *Vierteljahrshefte für Zeitgeschichte,* VI (January, 1958), 86–118.

Volz, Hans. *Daten der Geschichte der NSDAP.* Berlin & Leipzig: A. G. Plotz, 1934.

Vossische Zeitung, 1931, 1934.

Waite, Robert G. L. *Vanguard of Nazism.* Cambridge, Mass.: Harvard University Press, 1952.

Weber, Max. *The Theory of Social and Economic Organization,* trans. by A. M. Henderson and Talcott Parsons, ed. Talcott Parsons. New York: Oxford University Press, 1947.

Wendt, Hans. *Hitler Regiert,* 3rd ed. Berlin: E. S. Miller, 1933.

Wirth, Louis. "Ideological Aspects of Social Disorganization," *American Sociological Review,* V (August, 1940), 472–482.

Woodward, E. C., and R. Butler, eds. *Documents on British Foreign Policy 1919–1939;* 2nd series, Vols. IV–VI. London: H.M.S.O., 1950–1957.

Index